Life Changing Journey

750 Inspirational Quotes

SERIES IX

"Unveiling Wisdom: Inspiring Quotes to Spark Your Life. A Treasury of Inspiration for Cultivating Positivity on Life, Love, Nature, and More."

SHREE SHAMBAV

Life Changing Journey – Series IX
750 Inspirational Quotes
Shree Shambav

Published by Shree Shambav, Tamil Nadu, India

All Rights Reserved

First Edition, 2025

Copyright © 2025, Muniswamy Rajakumar

All rights reserved. No part of this publication may be reproduced, distributed, or transmitted in any form or by any means, including photocopying, recording, or other electronic or mechanical methods, without the author's prior written permission. It is illegal to copy this book, post it to a website, or distribute it by any other means without permission.

The request for permission should be addressed to the author.

ISBN: 978-93-343-2025-1

Email:shreeshambav@gmail.com

Web:www.shambav.org

DEDICATION

"Isavasyam idam sarvam yat kim ca jagatyam jagat, tena tyaktena bhunjitha, ma gridhah kasyasvid dhanam"

To the Almighty,

the Divine Masters,

the family who listens,

and my parents who see –

your presence shapes the pages of my life's journey.

"Isavasyam idam sarvam yat kim ca jagatyam jagat"

Meaning: "God encompasses everything you perceive, see, or touch with your sense organs."

DISCLAIMER

This book, *"Life-Changing Journey - Inspirational Quotes: Series IX,"* is a heartfelt compilation of personal reflections and insights born from the author's journey of understanding life and the natural world. Each inspirational quote is a subjective truth—a distillation of experience and thought—meant to serve as a mirror for readers to explore their own perspectives and uncover meaning through the lens of their unique experiences.

The intention behind this book is to share a message imbued with compassion, love, and care. It is designed to inspire readers on their personal journeys and guide them toward discovering the deeper realities of life. This is not a prescriptive manual but an invitation to pause, reflect, and engage with life's profound yet simple truths.

It's important to acknowledge that neither the content nor the sequence of the quotes is intended to cause harm, discomfort, or conflict with the reader's personal beliefs. Should any part of the book feel unsettling or contradictory to one's convictions, it is purely coincidental and never intentional.

The journey through these quotes is one of openness and fluidity, free from rigid interpretations or dogmatic assertions. The content reflects the author's personal perspective, humbly offered as a source of inspiration and gentle guidance. Readers are invited to engage with the material at their own pace, to reflect deeply, and to adapt the wisdom within to align with their inner truths and life experiences.

Above all, this book aspires to spark joy, nurture connection, and encourage purposeful living. It gently beckons readers to cultivate a life rooted in compassion, integrity, and intentionality while embracing the beauty of each moment with grace and mindfulness. May the words within these pages illuminate your path as you embark on a transformative journey of self-discovery, growth, and renewal. The journey is uniquely yours, and it is an honour for the author to accompany you, even if only in spirit, as you navigate the unfolding of your life.

With this understanding, readers are encouraged to approach the book with an open mind and heart, recognising that its wisdom is offered not as universal truth but as a collection of insights shaped by the author's personal experiences. You are invited to absorb what resonates, reinterpret what feels unfamiliar, and find your own meaning within these words.

Ultimately, the author's deepest wish is that these reflections serve as a beacon of hope, a source of motivation, and a catalyst for positivity as you embark on your life-changing journey. May this book inspire you to walk your path with courage, grace, and an unwavering belief in the beauty of life's unfolding.

Note - If any part of the book, in any sequence, hurts the reader's sentiments, it would be just out of a sheer accident, not intentional

Sacred Surrender

In the tender embrace of surrender lies the most profound revelation—the raw, unspoken beauty of union beyond all comprehension. It is in letting go, not in striving, that the soul awakens to its truest nature. As each ripple of the river dances toward the vast unknown, it carries within it a whispered confession, a silent declaration of trust and belonging to something far greater than itself.

The river does not resist its journey; it flows, it yields, and in that ceaseless motion, it unveils its sacred destiny—to merge with the ocean, to become one with the infinite. So too does the soul, when it surrenders its illusions of separation, rediscover its timeless kinship with the Divine.

This surrender is no defeat—it is a sacred metamorphosis, an unfolding of unparalleled grace. The fragmented self dissolves into the whole, and in that divine dissolution, the soul does not vanish but becomes vast. It transcends boundaries, shedding the illusions of ego to reveal the ineffable truth: that we are, and always have been, one with the Eternal.

In this divine act, the soul enters a sacred symphony—a silent, eternal melody echoing through the fabric of existence. It is the music of return, the sound of remembrance, the call home to a place we never truly left. Here, in the stillness beyond striving, we touch eternity. And in that sacred union, we are found.

– Shree Shambav

EPIGRAM

In the silence between thoughts, wisdom blooms.
In the stillness of the soul, the journey begins.
One quote, one breath, one awakening at a time—
Life transforms from within.

– Shree Shambav

Life Changing Journey

750 Inspirational Quotes

Shree Shambav

Shree Shambav is a 39x best-selling author renowned for his transformative works in personal development and spiritual growth.

Dear Cherished Readers

Dear Cherished Readers,

As I embark on this new literary voyage, my heart swells with profound gratitude and an overwhelming sense of connection. With deep emotion, I extend my heartfelt appreciation to each of you who has joined me on this journey.

With sincere warmth, I invite you to revisit the steps we have taken together through the pages of my earlier works. Our odyssey began with "Journey of Soul - Karma," a book that marked my first foray into the world of words and a testament to the raw passion that ignited my writing adventure.

The subsequent chapters of our shared narrative unfolded through the enchanting tapestry of the "Twenty + One" series. Each page turned was a brushstroke on the canvas of our imaginations, painting vivid stories that I hoped would resonate deeply within your hearts.

And how can I forget the transformative journey we embarked on with the "Life Changing Journey - Inspirational Quotes Series." Day by day, quote by quote, we delved into reflections that uplifted, inspired, and sought to bring a glimpse of light to our souls.

The release of "Death - Light of Life and the Shadow of Death" promises to shed new light on the timeless mystery of death.

The **Optimum Python Series** is a comprehensive guide designed to empower readers at every stage of their programming journey. It begins with *Series I: Ultimate Guide for Beginners*, which lays a strong foundation in Python, making it accessible and engaging for newcomers. *Series II: Exploring Data Structures and Algorithms* takes the next step, offering a deep dive into core computer science principles that enhance problem-solving skills and coding efficiency. Building on this, *Series III: Python Power for Data Science* introduces powerful libraries such as NumPy, Pandas, Matplotlib, and Scikit-learn, guiding readers through data manipulation, visualisation, and foundational machine learning techniques. Finally, *Series IV: Unleashing the Potential of Data Science with Machine Learning Techniques* explores advanced machine learning models and real-world applications, enabling readers to harness the full potential of data-driven insights. Whether you're just starting out or looking to master sophisticated tools and strategies, this series is your roadmap to Python proficiency and beyond.

Shree Shambav expands his artistic repertoire with *"Whispers of Eternity: 150 Plus - A Symphony of Soulful Verses,"* a heartfelt exploration of the human experience. Alongside this, his *"Whispers of the Soul: A Journey Through Haiku"* distils profound insights into poignant verses. Together, these works showcase his versatility and mastery of soulful expression, inviting readers on a journey of self-discovery. Through his poetry, he weaves a rich tapestry of emotion that resonates deeply with the heart.

LIFE CHANGING JOURNEY

Shree Shambav's latest works—*Learn to Love Yourself: A Journey of Discovering Inner Beauty and Strength Through 10 Transformative Rules, The Power of Letting Go: Embrace Freedom and Happiness, A Journey of Lasting Peace*—are true treasures of self-discovery, *The Entitlement Trap: Get Over It, Get On, Whispers of a Dying Soul: Unspoken Regrets and Unlived Dreams, Whispers of Silence - Unlocking Inner Power through Stillness, The Power of Words: Transforming Speech, Transforming Lives, The Art of Intentional Living: Minimalism for a Life of Purpose, Awakening the Infinite:The Power of Consciousness in Transforming Life, Beyond the Veil: A Journey Through Life After Death series, Bonds Beyond Blood - Where love builds bridges, and bonds defy blood., A Journey into Spiritual Maturity - 12 Golden Rules for Inner Transformation, The Seeker's Gold: Unlocking Life's Greatest Treasure and The Power of Manifestation - Unlocking The Path From Thought To Reality.*

In addition to these works, Shree Shambav has recently ventured into astrology with the release of Astrology Unveiled – Foundations of Ancient Wisdom Series I to VIII, expanding into the realm of metaphysics. These books explore the foundational principles of Vedic astrology, offering readers a rich and practical understanding of this ancient wisdom.

Your unwavering support, enthusiasm to immerse yourself in my writings, and readiness to embark on these journeys with me have been my greatest sources of inspiration. Your input has been a beacon guiding me through the creation process, moulding these stories into containers of passion, emotion, knowledge, and resonance.

As I unveil this new narrative before you, know that your presence, insights, and shared moments have been my companions. The path we have walked together is etched in the annals of my creative evolution, and it's an honour beyond words to have you by my side once more.

Here's to the readers who have illuminated my path with their presence, who have embraced my stories with open hearts, and who have woven themselves into the very fabric of my literary world. Our journey has been a symbiotic dance of writer and reader, a harmony of souls brought together by the magic of storytelling.

With a heart brimming with appreciation and eyes glistening with anticipation, I extend my deepest gratitude for your unwavering support. Thank you for the memories, the shared emotions, and the countless hours spent in the worlds we've crafted together. As we step into this new adventure, let's continue to explore, feel, and discover the boundless horizons that words can unveil.

Warmly,

Shree Shambav

LIFE CHANGING JOURNEY

Suggested Reads

FROM BEST-SELLING AUTHOR

Endorsements

"Life Changing Journey – Inspirational Quotes Series by Shree Shambav is more than just a book—it is a sacred offering to the soul. With rare poetic grace and spiritual clarity, Shambav distills profound truths into elegantly simple quotes that resonate like ancient mantras. Each page is a mirror reflecting the reader's inner light, reminding us that transformation does not require complexity—only presence, awareness, and courage.

Whether you are in search of healing, direction, or daily inspiration, this book meets you exactly where you are. It whispers hope into broken places and breathes purpose into the ordinary. In a world hungry for meaning, Life Changing Journey is a timeless companion—gentle, grounding, and luminous. This is not just a collection of quotes—it is a journey home to the self."

- Nita

About the Author

Shree Shambav is an internationally acclaimed, best-selling author, inspirational speaker, artist, philanthropist, life coach, and entrepreneur. A world record holder, his deep passion for music led him to create soul-stirring albums, drawing inspiration from his celebrated poetry collection, Whispers of Eternity. His profound insights have sparked deep personal transformations, guiding countless individuals toward self-discovery, purposeful living, and authenticity.

With an extraordinary ability to unlock human potential, Shree empowers individuals to break through limitations and embrace their highest selves. His writings, lectures, and compassionate guidance continue to uplift lives, fostering resilience, mindfulness, and personal growth.

Shree Shambav is a 39x best-selling author celebrated for his profound contributions to personal development and spiritual growth.

Shree Shambav's literary journey took flight with the celebrated Journey of Soul - Karma, where he delved into the depths of human experience to unveil profound insights. Garnering recognition through multiple literature awards, his repertoire includes esteemed works, such as the Twenty + One Series and the enlightening Life Changing Journey series.

As a distinguished alumnus of the Indian Institute of Management and the National Institute of Technology, Shree Shambav brings a wealth of corporate acumen from his tenure in multinational corporations. His most recent publications, including Unveiling the Enigma, Death - Light of Life and the Shadow of Death and Optimum - Python Series I, Series II, Series III and Series IV, demonstrate his mastery of both the literary and technical spheres.

Shree Shambav expands his artistic repertoire with "*Whispers of Eternity: 150 Plus - A Symphony of Soulful Verses*," a heartfelt exploration of the human experience. Alongside this, his "*Whispers of the Soul: A Journey Through Haiku*" distils profound insights into poignant verses. Together, these works showcase his versatility and mastery of soulful expression, inviting readers on a journey of self-discovery. Through his poetry, he weaves a rich tapestry of emotion that resonates deeply with the heart.

Shree Shambav's latest works—*Learn to Love Yourself: A Journey of Discovering Inner Beauty and Strength Through 10 Transformative Rules, The Power of Letting Go: Embrace Freedom and Happiness, A*

LIFE CHANGING JOURNEY

Journey of Lasting Peace—are true treasures of self-discovery, The Entitlement Trap: Get Over It, Get On, Whispers of a Dying Soul: Unspoken Regrets and Unlived Dreams, Whispers of Silence - Unlocking Inner Power through Stillness, The Power of Words: Transforming Speech, Transforming Lives, The Art of Intentional Living: Minimalism for a Life of Purpose, Awakening the Infinite:The Power of Consciousness in Transforming Life, Beyond the Veil: A Journey Through Life After Death series, Bonds Beyond Blood - Where love builds bridges, and bonds defy blood., A Journey into Spiritual Maturity - 12 Golden Rules for Inner Transformation, The Seeker's Gold: Unlocking Life's Greatest Treasure and The Power of Manifestation - Unlocking The Path From Thought To Reality.

In addition to these works, Shree Shambav has recently ventured into astrology with the release of Astrology Unveiled – Foundations of Ancient Wisdom Series I to VIII, expanding into the realm of metaphysics. These books explore the foundational principles of Vedic astrology, offering readers a rich and practical understanding of this ancient wisdom.

Shree Shambav established the Ayur Rakshita Foundation, which is dedicated to promoting boundless growth, universal fraternity, and environmental protection. The charity helps diverse communities while working for societal progress.

To learn more about Shree Shambav and his works, visit his website at www.shambav.org. For information about the Ayur Rakshita Foundation and its initiatives, visit www.shambav-ayurrakshita.org.

Let's Follow him on Social Media: **@shreeshambav**

Main: https://linktr.ee/shreeshambav

SHREE SHAMBAV

Website: https://www.shambav.org/

LinkedIn: https://www.linkedin.com/in/shreeshambav/

Blog: https://blog.shambav.org/

Instagram: https://www.instagram.com/shreeshambav/

YouTube: https://www.youtube.com/@shreeshambav

Amazon: https://www.amazon.com/author/shreeshambav

Goodreads: https://www.goodreads.com/author/show/22367436.Shree_Shambav

PREFACE

Life is a symphony—each moment a unique note, resonating within the grand composition of existence. Amid this unfolding melody, words hold a timeless and transformative power: they awaken, heal, and uplift. *Life Changing Journey – Inspirational Quotes Series* by Shree Shambav is far more than a compilation of quotes—it is a soulful companion, a luminous guide, and a steadfast beacon for those navigating the intricate pathways of life.

This book was born in moments of quiet reflection—when the noise of the world fades and the soul begins to speak. Each quote distills universal truths into expressions that are both simple and profound—echoes of human experience captured in words. Through these pages, you are invited to embark on a journey of introspection, awakening, and transformation.

The chapters are intentionally crafted, each one offering a thematic exploration of the human spirit. They illuminate the courage to embrace change, the strength to pursue dreams, and the grace to find meaning amidst adversity. With gentle wisdom, they speak of love and connection, of the beauty found in self-acceptance, and of the quiet resilience that lies dormant within us all. They remind us of the joy in simplicity, the awakening of gratitude through mindfulness, and the sacred harmony between humanity, nature, and the cosmos.

This series is a tapestry woven from timeless insights that transcend time and circumstance. It invites you to pause and reflect, to draw inspiration from within and from the shared wisdom of generations. Whether you are weathering life's storms, seeking clarity, or longing for peace, these words will meet you where you are—offering light, comfort, and renewed strength.

Each volume in the series unfolds a unique dimension of human experience:

- **Series II** beautifully weaves together timeless themes such as self-discovery, dreams and aspirations, embracing change and imperfections, inner strength, gratitude, mindfulness, inspiration, and resilience. It explores love, relationships, the harmony of nature, the pursuit of purpose, serenity, and balance. Through reflections on simplicity, kindness, spiritual connection, and age-old wisdom, this series offers heartfelt guidance for every stage of life's journey."

- **Series III** explores *Embracing Change, Discovering Self, Dreams and Aspirations, Embracing Imperfections, Finding Inner Strength,* and *Gratitude and Mindfulness*—prompting deep reflection on personal growth, identity, and soulful resilience.

- **Series IV** delves into *Inspiration and Motivation, Lessons from Adversity, Love and Relationships, Nature's Symphony, Pursuing Your Dreams,* and *Serenity and Balance*—guiding readers toward purpose, harmony, and deeper emotional connection.

- **Series V** journeys through *Shades of Existence, Success and Achievement, The Beauty of Simplicity, The Power of Kindness,* and *Wisdom from the Ages*—reminding us to find strength in timeless truths and joy in life's simplest moments.

- **Series VI** culminates in a journey of inner stillness and soulful reflection through *Embracing Change, Love and Relationships, Serenity and Balance, Shades of Existence,* and *Whispers of the Divine.* These themes gently invite us to slow down, listen deeply, and recognise the sacred in everyday life.

- **Series VII** deepens this introspection, guiding us through *Discovering the Self, Finding Inner Strength, Lessons from Adversity, The Power of Kindness,* and *Wisdom from the Ages*—offering clarity, healing, and courage born of compassion.

- **Series VIII** touches the heart of human experience with *Embracing Change, Embracing Imperfections, Finding Inner Strength, Gratitude and Mindfulness, Inspiration and Motivation, Nature's Symphony, Shades of Existence,* and *The Beauty of Simplicity*—a celebration of authenticity, resilience, and soulful living.

- **Series IX** continues this profound journey with *Discovering Self, Finding Inner Strength, Inspiration and*

Motivation, Nature's Symphony, Pursuing Your Dreams, Success and Achievement, and *Wisdom from the Ages*—a radiant culmination of inner transformation and meaningful action.

Rooted in mindfulness, gratitude, and inspiration, these volumes nurture quiet resilience and clarity. Through nature's rhythms and life's enduring truths, they remind us that lasting transformation begins within.

These chapters are lanterns on the path of growth—illuminating how hardship refines us, how kindness transforms, and how the wisdom of those who walked before us still echoes with relevance today. They remind us that every challenge holds a lesson, and every moment offers a choice to awaken.

Shree Shambav's words transcend the mundane, touching the sacred essence of life. They serve as gentle reminders of our shared humanity, encouraging us to embrace imperfection, live authentically, and rediscover the divine spark within. Each quote is a spark—a catalyst for growth and self-discovery, illuminating the way through life's trials and triumphs.

As you turn these pages, may you discover not just inspiration but connection—to yourself, to others, and to the beauty that surrounds you. Let this book be your sanctuary of wisdom, a reservoir of courage, and a wellspring of hope. Let it remind you that you are not alone on this journey.

Welcome to the *Life Changing Journey – Inspirational Quotes Series*. May this book inspire you to live boldly, love deeply, and awaken the boundless joy within your own journey.

With heartfelt gratitude and encouragement,
Shree Shambav

INTRODUCTION

In every human life, there comes a moment—a pause between heartbeats—when we ask ourselves the deeper questions: *Who am I beyond the roles I play? Why am I here? What is the meaning of this journey I am walking?* These questions are not signs of doubt; they are the soul's quiet invitation to awaken.

Life Changing Journey – Inspirational Quotes Series was born from that space of inner stillness, where truth whispers, where insight dawns, and where even a single sentence can shift a life's direction. This book is not merely a compilation of words—it is a mirror, a lantern, and a companion for all who dare to reflect, evolve, and walk consciously through the labyrinth of existence.

We live in a time of great noise—externally through distraction and internally through self-doubt, fear, and the pressure to perform. But amidst the chaos, the human spirit remains unbroken. Within every heart lies a quiet reservoir of courage, a longing to be seen, and a spark waiting to be ignited. This collection of inspirational quotes is designed to reach into that inner space to awaken clarity, rekindle purpose, and soothe the parts of us that feel unseen or unheard.

Each quote is crafted not only with poetic precision but with soulful intent. Some may arrive as gentle reminders, others as fierce awakenings. They touch on the universal themes that unite us all—change, love, imperfection, resilience, gratitude, connection, and the silent wisdom of nature. They are arranged in a way that guides the reader through stages of transformation—from awakening and acceptance to action, reflection, and inner peace.

This book is for the seeker and the silent warrior, the dreamer and the doer, the broken and the brave. It is for anyone who has stumbled, doubted, loved deeply, lost profoundly, or stood at the edge of change. It is for those who carry quiet questions in their hearts and those who find comfort in a single sentence that speaks to their soul.

You do not have to read this book in order. Let it be a companion you can return to at any moment—open to any page, and you may just find the words you didn't know you needed. Let each chapter be a sacred pause, a deep breath, a turning inward.

As you journey through these words, may you rediscover the beauty of your own truth. May you remember that the answers you seek are not far—they live within you, waiting to rise. Let this be your quiet revolution—one thought, one quote, one heartbeat at a time.

Welcome to the *Life Changing Journey*.

Your soul already knows the way.

With warmth and sincerity,

Shree Shambav

PROLOGUE

The Silence Between the Words

There is a moment before dawn when the world holds its breath—a sacred stillness, where light has not yet broken, but darkness has already begun to soften. It is in this tender silence that something ancient stirs within us—a quiet knowing that we are more than the stories we tell, more than the burdens we carry, more than the fears we hide behind a smile.

In that space, words are not just language. They become messengers. Carriers of hope. Fragments of truth passed down through lifetimes, echoing the wisdom of countless souls who have walked the path before us.

Life Changing Journey – Inspirational Quotes Series is born from that silence.

It is not simply a book, but a gathering of sacred reflections—each quote a droplet of insight, each chapter a river leading inward. It does not seek to teach, but to remind. To gently awaken what has always lived within you: your strength, your beauty, your inner clarity. The unshakable truth that you are whole, even in your brokenness. That you are loved, even in your silence.

This series is a mirror—not to your outer life, but to the inner landscapes of your soul. It meets you in your loneliness and offers light. It sits with you in your uncertainty and brings presence. It walks beside you through joy and sorrow alike, not promising answers, but offering resonance.

The quotes in these pages were not written in haste. They were breathed into being—each one drawn from moments of stillness, wonder, grief, gratitude, and revelation. They carry the rhythm of the cosmos, the heartbeat of the Earth, and the timeless voice of the spirit.

As you open this book, do not rush. Let the words find you. Let them fall where they must. You may not remember them all, but some will stay—etched not on paper, but on the walls of your soul. Those are the ones that were always meant for you.

So take a breath. Let go of who you were supposed to be.

Enter this space as you are—raw, real, human, divine.

You are not here by accident. This moment was always waiting for you.

Let the journey begin.

– Shree Shambav

Welcome to *The Life-Changing Journey – Inspirational Quotes Series.*

CONTENTS

DEDICATION iii
DISCLAIMER v
Sacred Surrender vii
EPIGRAM ix
Dear Cherished Readers xiii
Suggested Reads xvii
Endorsements xix
About the Author xxi
PREFACE xxv
INTRODUCTION xxxi
PROLOGUE xxxiii
Discovering Self 1
   Reflections on Identity and Purpose 1
Finding Inner Strength 27
   Empowering the Mind and Spirit 27
Inspiration and Motivational 57
   Fuelling the Soul 57
Nature Symphony 93
   Odes to the Earth 93
Pursuing your Dreams 135
   Overcoming Obstacles 135
Success and Achievements 153
   Unleashing Your Potential 153

Wisdom of Ages 181
   Timeless Insights for Life 181
Life Coach and Philanthropist 209
TESTIMONIALS 211
ACKNOWLEDGEMENTS 219

Discovering Self

Reflections on Identity and Purpose

"I searched the world to find who I am, only to learn—my purpose was never something to chase, but something I was meant to remember. Not in the mirror, but in the quiet places where my soul first learned to whisper its truth."

- Shree Shambav

A Masterpiece in Motion

"With each passing moment, we don't just live—we create. Our love is a masterpiece rendered by soul, not hand."

Alignment Is Peace

"Peace is what happens when your life stops arguing with your soul."

Awakened Alignment

"When mind and body move as one, the impossible begins to look effortless."

Beauty Misunderstood

"We chase beauty as appearance, and miss it as presence."

Becoming Whole Again

"Healing isn't about returning to who you were. It's becoming who you were meant to be."

Before the Shift

"Before trying to change your mind, learn to understand it. Awareness is the first act of transformation."

Beyond the Ledger

"Life is not a balance sheet of pleasures and pains, but the courage to keep walking through both."

Beyond the Mask

"The world may praise the mask, but only your soul knows when you're pretending."

Blossoms Come Later

"The bloom is never the first gift. Rain, patience, and darkness come first."

Burn Bright, Not Fast

"The flame that endures is not the one that dazzles, but the one that warms."

Calm is Earned

"You have learned calmness not through escape, but through meeting the storm and staying still within it."

Canvas of Choice

"Every choice is a brushstroke; paint with intention, and your life becomes a masterpiece."

Canvas of Us

"The world is a canvas, and with every brushstroke of love, we turn the ordinary into art—together."

Clarity Over Closure

"Some chapters don't need closure. They need clarity, distance, and a softer heart."

Consistency Is the Real Talent

"Genius fades. Charisma flickers. But consistency compounds."

Decade Thinking

"Think in decades, act in days. That's how legacies are built."

Endlessly Told

"Our love isn't a moment—it's a story the stars still whisper, a tale without ending, written hand in hand."

Essence Over Impression

"Leave behind the chase for attention—return to the craft of essence."

Focus is Devotion

"Each task deserves your full energy. Attention is the soul's way of saying—this matters."

Freedom in Surrender

"Surrender isn't giving up—it's giving in to truth, where real strength lives."

From Seed to Self

"Every belief you plant becomes a root in the body you live in."

From Want to Will

"Desire asks for more. Love asks, 'What can I give?' In that shift, healing begins."

Full Presence, Full Potential

"Whether in work or in love, give fully. Half-hearted presence creates echoes, not impact."

Gratitude for the Dark

"Be grateful for the nights you wanted to quit. They're the reason you shine now."

Gratitude's Bloom

"Let go of what you're owed, and gratitude will blossom in the garden of your being."

Grief Is a Teacher

"Grief is not the enemy of joy—it's what clears the space for joy to be felt fully."

Harmony Within

"When the mind is still, the body acts with purpose. When the mind is scattered, the body echoes its chaos."

Healing as Return

"Healing is not a battle to win. It's a homecoming to love."

Inner Architecture

"You don't build a life around achievements. You build it around alignment."

Inward First, Outward Next

"A still mind leads the way; the body only follows. Victory begins in silence, not sound."

Leadership in Rain

"Leaders are not made in applause—they are shaped in silence and storm."

Love as Language

"Tell your body it is loved. It has waited years to hear it from you."

Melody for Two

"Every heartbeat is a song that no one else can hear—a melody written in the silence between us."

Poverty of Self

"True poverty isn't lack of money. It's forgetting who you are."

Power Redefined

"Power is not how loudly you speak, but how deeply your silence is respected."

Presence Over Performance

"The most radical success is showing up as yourself, without needing to impress."

Purpose in the Pain

"Sometimes the ache isn't asking to be fixed—it's asking to be heard."

Rain Teaches Roots

"The roots don't grow in sunshine—they deepen in rain, unseen but enduring."

Rain as a Gift

"Not all storms come to break you. Some come to the water what you prayed for."

Reclaiming the Inner Voice

"When you stop living to be understood, you begin living to understand."

Reflection Creates Clarity

"When you reflect with sincerity, answers arrive not rushed—but right on time, and crystal clear."

Return to the Body

"Your body isn't your enemy. It's the journal where your soul wrote its survival."

Rhythm of Two

"In the quiet symmetry of our steps, through storm or shine, our rhythm remains—soft, steady, and true."

Sacred No

"Every time you say 'no' to what drains you, you say 'yes' to who you're becoming."

Scarred Into Wisdom

"Some pain doesn't pass through you—it stays, carves, and becomes part of the shape that makes you wise."

Soul Debt

"Every time you betray your truth for approval, your soul takes on a debt only courage can repay."

Stagnation in Silence

"Meditation without movement is sleep. Insight must meet action to become transformation."

Still Waters, Deep Wisdom

"There is power in stillness. Reflection is where clarity begins and intention becomes strength."

Stillness into Action

"Stillness is not inactivity—it is preparation. From it rises action that is focused, grounded, and whole."

Surrender Over Striving

"Not everything must be fought. Some things heal when you stop resisting."

The Alchemy of Struggle

"Hard seasons don't steal your worth—they refine it."

The Art of Letting Go

"Letting go is not giving up. It's returning the weight to the sky and walking free with grace."

The Clarity of Less

"Simplify your focus—not because you're doing less, but because less brings more into sharp view."

The Courage to Be

"True courage lies in embracing the vulnerability of the present, knowing that every moment is a thread in the tapestry of forever."

The Currency of Presence

"Time isn't a gift. Presence is. One can be spent. The other can only be given."

The Dance of Time

"Time is not a thief but a dance partner. When you move with grace and presence, it leads you to moments of infinite beauty."

The Eternal Echo

"Every act of love echoes across lifetimes, a melody carried by the winds of eternity."

The Eternal Thread

"Each life is a thread in the fabric of existence, woven together to create a tapestry that spans eternity."

The Flight of Heart

"When you walk beside me, my heart forgets the ground—love becomes the wings I never knew I had."

The Flow of Life

"Embrace the flow—resistance turns rivers into floods, but surrender shapes them into harmony."

The Garden Within

"Tend to your inner world like soil. What you believe, feel, and feed—grows."

The Garden's Whisper

"Your body hears everything you think. Speak like someone planting a garden, not fixing a machine."

The Gift of Emptiness

"In the emptiness of the moment lies the fullness of life. Embrace it, and you will find everything you need."

The Gift of Now

"The present moment is a doorway to eternity; step through it with love, for it is all we truly ever have."

The Hue of Forever

"Let's paint the sky in colours only our hearts can see—because forever is not a time, it's a feeling we share."

The Illusion of More

"Owning more means nothing if you feel less at home in yourself."

The Infinite Within

"The universe you seek lies within you. To journey inward is to discover the infinite in the depths of your soul."

The Invisible Riches

"If you can sleep with peace and wake with purpose, you are already wealthy."

The Law of Invisible Growth

"What doesn't show up today might be growing roots beneath the surface. Compound wisely."

The Leader's Silence

"Leadership isn't loud. It begins in quiet choices no one claps for."

The Light Within

"The soul is like a lamp in the dark; no storm can extinguish it, for its flame is lit by the eternal."

The Measure of a Life

"A life well-lived is not measured by years, but by the depth of love shared, the kindness given, and the joy created."

The Mirror Beyond the Face

"You are not what the mirror shows. You are the one watching quietly behind the eyes."

The Mirror of Silence

"Silence is a mirror that reflects the truth of your soul. Gaze into it, and you will see the infinite within yourself."

The Monk's Precision

"He moves like a Shaolin monk—not rushed, not delayed, but precise. Because every act is sacred."

The Most Loyal Listener

"Your body listens closer than anyone else ever will. Speak to it with devotion."

The Myth of Arrival

"Peace doesn't wait at the finish line. It walks with those who choose presence over pace."

The Power of One

"Success is not in doing a hundred things at once—but in doing one thing with your full presence."

The Power of Presence

"Success that costs your presence is just another form of absence."

The Queen Within

"You weren't born to serve someone else's idea of worth. You were meant to rise."

The Quietest Knowing

"Some truths don't shout—they settle in your bones and wait for you to listen."

The Return to Self

"In a world that sells you versions of yourself, wholeness is the act of returning home to the original."

The Root of Thought

"You cannot change your thoughts until you become aware of them. Observation is the beginning of choice."

The Scar's Wisdom

"Wounds don't only hurt—they remember, reshape, and remind us we survived."

The Sky of the Heart

"The heart is a vast sky, where even the darkest clouds are temporary and the light of love is always present."

The Soul's Compass

"If success costs you your peace, then it was never aligned with your purpose."

The Soul's Journey

"The soul's journey is not a straight line but a spiral, each turn bringing us closer to the center of who we are."

The Soul's True Wealth

"The richest life isn't filled with things—it's aligned with truth."

The Story Awaits

"The world is not waiting to serve your expectations—it is waiting to be transformed by your awakening."

The Sweet Snare

"Entitlement speaks in honeyed tones, yet binds the spirit tighter than any visible chain."

The Treasure of Simplicity

"Simplicity is not the absence of ambition but the presence of clarity—a return to what truly matters."

The Weight of Blame

"Blame is the warmest prison—a shelter that stifles the soul's rise."

The Weight of Love

"Love is the only burden worth carrying, for it grows lighter with each step, and leaves joy in its path."

The Weight of Masks

"We lose more of ourselves pretending to be strong than we ever do by being vulnerable."

The Whisper of Eternity

"Eternity speaks not in shouts, but in whispers—the quiet moments where love, presence, and truth intersect."

The Wisdom in Waiting

"Not all stillness is stagnation. Sometimes, it's the soil preparing for a deeper bloom."

Truth Has No Price Tag

"A life aligned with truth is richer than one adorned with trophies."

Truth as Medicine

"Sometimes the cure isn't in the pill. It's in finally telling yourself the truth."

Unseen Practice, Visible Power

"Quiet moments of practice shape bold moments of action. Stillness trains the storm."

What Storms Awaken

"You don't know how strong your roots are until the rain comes."

Wholeness Isn't Perfection

"Healing doesn't make you flawless. It makes you whole."

Finding Inner Strength

Empowering the Mind and Spirit

"The mind awakens when it questions fear, but the spirit rises when it remembers its light. True power is not control—but the quiet clarity that comes when thought and soul walk hand in hand."

- *Shree Shambav*

A Life Without Expectation

"To live without expectation is not to be empty, but to be full of what is real."

A Promise Across Paths

"Even when roads diverge, love honours the journey we once walked together."

Becoming the Message

"The world doesn't need more content. It needs more people whose lives have become their message."

Beyond the Seen

"To love is to see without eyes, to believe beyond sight, and to feel without form."

Designing Destiny

"Destiny isn't found—it's designed, moment by moment, through what you tolerate, cultivate, and celebrate."

Echoes in the Night

"When all else falls away, we meet ourselves not in triumph, but in quiet, aching truth."

Echoes of You

"Memories are not remnants of the past, but rivers that still carry your laughter into my now."

Echoes of the Unseen

"The world honours what's visible—but your soul knows your rise began the moment you chose the unseen work."

Equal in the Sunlight

"The sun makes no distinction; it warms the wings of all who dare to rise."

Fall as a Teacher

"Your fall was not a failure. It was gravity guiding you back to the ground of your own authenticity."

Forged by Fire

"In the furnace of trials, we are not destroyed but refined—tempered into something unbreakable."

Forward With Grace

"We rise by embracing our past—not to dwell, but to walk forward with deeper grace."

Freedom with Roots

"Real freedom isn't escape—it's the deep anchoring into who you are, so nothing outside can own you."

Freedom's Nature

"Real freedom is not escape from the world, but the art of living lightly within it."

From Earth to Illusion

"We rise from soil to summit, only to find that the peak was never ours to keep."

Glow Through the Storm

"Let the storms come—your light was never meant to hide, but to shine through the rain."

Grace Beyond All Loss

"When we surrender all, what is left is grace — eternal, unwavering, and profoundly ours."

Grace in the Grit

"Even in life's muddiest trials, grace grows quietly, like a lotus pushing through pain."

Healers of the Wild

"What medicine can match the healing found in a life lived close to the earth?"

Healing Through Rhythm

"Even the broken body heals in rhythm. So too, your soul—through sacred routines and meaningful rituals."

Healing from Within

"Time does not heal wounds; it merely reveals that healing was always waiting within us."

Healing is Intelligence

"The choice to heal isn't weakness—it's the highest form of emotional intelligence."

Hope's Quiet Bloom

"Even when lost in darkness, hope plants roots in silence and grows toward unseen light."

Intimacy with the Unknown

"Great lives are not built on certainty. They are forged in intimacy with the unknown."

Legacy Beyond Achievement

"The real legacy isn't in what you built, but in who you became while building."

Lessons at the Crossroads

"Every uncertain path is an invitation to grow into the courage we silently hold."

Longing's Question

"The heart, in its silence, often asks what the lips dare not — does the soul I seek, seek me too?"

Nature's Message

"Every bird that sings and breeze that stirs becomes the voice of a love that refuses to fade."

Presence as Power

"You don't need more time—you need more presence in the time you already have."

Pride's Silent Collapse

"Armies fall not for lack of power, but from the weight of their own unyielding pride."

Purpose in the Storm

"True strength is not found in resisting the storm but in standing still long enough to understand its purpose."

Rebirth Through Ruin

"Within despair lies a quiet power, waiting to become the strength of our rebirth."

Rise and Radiate

"Life's struggles do not define who you are—they reveal who you are becoming."

Root Before Rise

"You cannot rise sustainably until you root unapologetically—into truth, into values, into self."

Sacred Discomfort

"Growth doesn't always feel like expansion—it often feels like sacred discomfort asking for your stretch."

Stillness is Strategy

"In a world addicted to urgency, stillness isn't laziness—it's leadership."

Strength in Absence

"True love does not wane in absence; it becomes the very light that defies the dark."

Strength in Shadows

"In the darkest chapters of life, we uncover the light we didn't know we carried."

Success Without Soul is Noise

"Success without soul is performance. But when spirit leads, even your silence becomes impact."

The Alchemy of Suffering

"Suffering is not the end but the crucible where the soul is transformed, forged into a vessel for wisdom and compassion."

The Art of Becoming

"You are not a product of your past. You are the artist of your becoming—each moment a fresh canvas of choice."

The Art of Surrender

"Growth is not in the reaching but in the surrender—letting go of who we think we are to become who we were meant to be."

The Blindfold of Progress

"In building towers to the sky, we forget the sky was already ours to begin with."

The Blooming Within

"In life's tangled maze, strength isn't found—it unfolds from within, one step at a time."

The Boundary of Becoming

"Boundaries are not walls. They are sacred definitions of where you stop abandoning yourself."

The Climb Within

"Every uphill battle is not just a test of endurance—it's a revelation of the strength you didn't know you carried."

The Company You Keep

"The circles you sit in will either reflect your limitations or awaken your liberation."

The Crucible Truth

"It is only when we walk through the fire that we remember we were born of stars."

The Dance of Destiny

"We may part ways, but true connections echo across time, aligned in unseen ways."

The Deep Currency of Energy

"The energy you carry speaks before you enter the room. Make your presence your true portfolio."

The Divine Realisation

"In the stillness beyond sorrow, the soul whispers: what I sought outside was always You."

The Eternal Embrace

"God is not a distant force, but the warmth we remember when the world grows cold."

The Eternal Wait

"Devotion, when true, does not count the days — it only trusts that love will find its way back."

The Fire Beneath Failure

"Failure is not an ending. It is friction—the sacred heat that softens who you're not, to reveal who you are."

The Fire Within

"The fire of the soul does not burn to destroy but to illuminate the path through the darkness of fear and doubt."

The First Flight

"To be born is not enough; to rise and breathe in the morning sky is the soul's true beginning."

The Flame That Bends

"Be not the stone that stands cold and tall, but the flame that dances and endures through storm."

The Garden of Consciousness

"The garden you walk tomorrow grows from the soil of your current awareness — tend it with clarity and presence."

The Gentle Art of Becoming

"You are not racing toward a destination; you are slowly unfolding into the masterpiece you already are."

The Gentle Refrain

"Nature sings softly to those who listen—not with answers, but with peace."

The Grace of Sway

"The living bend and dance with the wind—those who cannot, wither where they stand."

The Hidden Gift

"Adversity is often a disguised invitation to meet your most resilient self."

The Humility of Vision

"A true visionary is not one who sees everything clearly—but one who walks forward despite not knowing."

The Illusion of Strength

"To appear unbreakable is not strength; true strength is found in the willingness to bend."

The Infinite in Stillness

"To embrace stillness is to touch the infinite; within the quiet lies a universe waiting to be explored."

The Inner Lighthouse

"When you become your own source of light, no storm can make you forget the shore within."

The Inner Parliament

"You cannot rise if your inner voices are at war. Peace within is the first law of outer alignment."

The Invisible Chains

"It is not gold but grasping that shackles us, not lack but longing that enslaves."

The Invisible Infrastructure

"The unseen disciplines—rest, reflection, alignment—are the scaffolding of a rise that sustains."

The Journey Within

"The greatest journeys are not those measured by miles but by the depths of transformation within."

The Joy in the Simple

"Happiness does not bloom in grandeur, but in the quiet grace of enough."

The Law of Open Hearts

"In the end, it's not power that governs, but hearts open enough to love through pain."

The Legacy Between Heartbeats

"Legacy isn't just what you leave behind. It's what your presence awakens in others, heartbeat by heartbeat."

The Mirage of Ownership

"What we clutch with pride often slips like sand — for nothing truly belongs but the love we give."

The Mirror of Relationships

"Every relationship is a mirror. Some show you who you were. The rare ones reveal who you're becoming."

The One Who Remains

"When every name fades, one remains — the Divine, the silent witness behind every gain and grief."

The Painted Mind

"Love, once felt, becomes a brush that endlessly colours the canvas of remembrance."

The Paradox of Life

"Life and death take turns in every breath—we die a little to learn how to live again."

The Power of Invisible Work

"That which no one sees—your inner shifts, your silent refusals, your late-night awakenings—are the foundation of your visible rise."

The Power of the Unwritten

"You are not bound by your backstory. You are liberated by the next word you dare to write in the silence of now."

The Pulse of Inner Wealth

"When you learn to feel rich in solitude, no external lack can rob you of peace."

The Pulse of Purpose

"Purpose isn't something you chase. It's something that pulses louder the quieter your ego becomes."

The Question of Permanence

"It is only in loss that we begin to ask what was real, and what merely glittered in our grasp."

The Quiet Rise

"You don't always ascend in the spotlight. Some of your greatest rises happen in rooms no one sees, in choices no one applauds."

The Quiet Wait

"In the vast expanse of time, love teaches patience more than presence ever could."

The Resistance of Rigidity

"What resists the flow of life breaks not from weakness, but from the refusal to yield."

The Rhythm of Renewal

"Burnout is not about doing too much. It's about forgetting to return to rhythm—rest, reflection, return."

The Sacred Weight of Meaning

"Power without purpose corrodes. But when wealth is welded to meaning, it becomes medicine for generations."

The Sanctuary Within

"Build your inner world as a sanctuary—not a storage room of others' opinions."

The Silent Victory

"Sometimes, surviving the day is the loudest victory the heart can ever sing."

The Soft Beginning

"We enter this world supple and open, not to conquer it with might, but to feel it with wonder."

The Song of Simplicity

"In chasing what is rare, we forget that beauty lies where nothing needs to be earned."

The Soul Beyond Success

"It is not success or failure that defines us, but the soul we uncover in the in-between."

The Soul's Compass

"Your deepest desires are not selfish cravings — they are often compass needles pointing to karmic fulfilment."

The Space Between Chapters

"Don't rush the space between chapters. Sometimes, the silence between stories carries your greatest alignment."

The Surrendered Architect

"You are not here to force the future, but to become the kind of soul it naturally belongs to."

The Threshold of Trust

"Every next level of your life asks for a deeper level of trust—not in outcomes, but in essence."

The Throne of Ego

"He who crowns himself with wealth will one day bow to the silence it cannot fill."

The Vanishing Hand

"All we gather fades like a passing breeze — what endures cannot be held, only felt."

The Vanishing Light

"Some presences are like dusk — luminous and brief, but remembered long into the night."

The Warrior's Soul

"True strength is not in how loud we roar, but in how quietly we rise again after falling."

The Whisper of Wisdom

"Wisdom rarely arrives in noise; it speaks in pauses, in patterns, and in the spaces you once rushed through."

The Winding Road

"Life is not a straight path but a winding trail, where every twist teaches, and every turn unveils a truth."

The Wisdom of Softness

"In a world obsessed with power, softness remains the most radical form of resilience."

The Wisdom of Withdrawal

"Sometimes stepping away isn't quitting—it's recalibrating your soul's direction before your body collapses from the misalignment."

To Live is to Yield

"Living isn't about holding firm, but about flowing, changing, and still remaining true."

Unlearning to Begin Again

"Your rebirth doesn't begin with what you learn. It begins with what you are finally willing to unlearn."

Unseen Commitments

"The world measures results. The soul measures your invisible commitments—the ones that change your axis before they change your outcomes."

Whispers of Wisdom

"The mind moves forward with logic, but the heart lingers with purpose."

Wings of Mortality

"I may not soar like dreams do, but love gives flight to the grounded soul."

Inspiration and Motivational

Fuelling the Soul

The soul is not fed by noise or applause, but by the silent fire of purpose, the warmth of truth, and the gentle breath of meaning—where even the smallest act, done with love, becomes eternal nourishment."

- *Shree Shambav*

A Gift Too Brief

"Some angels walk this earth only for a while, just long enough to remind us what heaven feels like."

A Haven in the Storm

"In the quiet grace of love's embrace, even the fiercest storms become places of shelter."

A Kinder Dream

"From the gentlest tears bloom the kindest dreams—washed in grief, but rooted in love deeper than pain."

Alchemy of the Soul

"What fire consumes is not the self but the illusion; in the ashes, the truth gleams brighter than gold."

Beyond Fault and Shame

"In love's light, scars are not marks of failure, but the colours of resilience and truth."

Beyond the Mould

"Release the roles you've outgrown—what clung to you in the past cannot carry you into your wholeness."

Born of Night

"Some lights are not born of flame, but of shadow—taught to glow softly through the quiet art of surviving."

Carved by Silence

"In the hush after loss, something eternal whispers—what breaks you, also births you."

Cycles of the Heart

"The heart has its own lunar rhythm—waxing with love, waning with grief, yet always returning to light."

Echoes of Endings and Beginnings

"Every tear holds a farewell and a first step forward—grief and hope walking hand in hand through the night."

Echoes of Her Laughter

"Her laughter still lingers in the corners of my memory—soft, radiant, untouched by time, yet aching in absence."

Firewalk to Freedom

"Walking away from the need to prove is the first step toward peace that stays."

Flicker Before Dawn

"Even in the deepest night, a flicker of light reminds us that every ending holds a beginning."

Forever in the Eternal

"You are not lost—you are the silence in our prayers, the echo in our joy, and the eternal verse in our unfinished song."

Freedom from the Chase

"The freest soul is not the one who has it all, but the one no longer running after it."

Friendship as Light

"True friends are not beside you—they are within you, lighting paths you were afraid to walk alone."

From Battle to Garden

"Healing is not a war to win, but a garden tended with patience and gentle love."

Grace Walks Forward

"Grace never lingers in yesterday's shell—it beckons you into the fire that shapes you into yourself."

Grace in Poverty

"Poverty, held with grace, can reveal a strength that even empires envy."

Grains of Time

"Time slips like sand through trembling hands—each lost moment a silent lament of the heart."

Half-Lost, Half-Alive

"To remain unchanged is to live only halfway—to avoid the ache is to miss the miracle."

Held Beyond Doubt

"You are held beyond the reach of doubt—whole, unbroken, and radiant beneath the surface of all fears."

Hope in the Shadows

"Even the darkest night holds a silver glow—for where despair once slept, hope begins to bloom in secret."

Hope on the Windowsill

"Each evening, I sit by the window not to watch the world pass, but to hope she'll glance back—just once."

If Only She Knew

"If she ever wonders what she meant to me, I hope the wind carries my silent cry to where she walks."

Lessons of Regret

"Regret, when embraced, becomes a teacher—each pause a step toward redemption's grace."

Love That Rises

"Love rises gentle and unrelenting, folding us in its wings when we feel most alone."

Love's Ashes in the Storm

"She was taken too soon, yet in the arms of the storm, her presence returns—fierce, fleeting, and eternal."

Love's Healing Touch

"True love is the gentle balm that transforms hidden wounds into blossoms of grace."

Love's Quiet Cage

"There is no prison more painful than the one built from love unspoken and time misused."

Made for More

"You are not meant for the shrinking shore—your soul is carved for open seas and unseen stars."

Miles Can't Mend the Soul

"You can cross oceans in search of self, but no journey heals what truth denies."

Mist of the Mind

"Thoughts rise like morning mist, beautiful yet brief—disappearing when touched by the clarity of presence."

Moonlit Confessions

"Beneath the moon's quiet watch, the heart tells truths no voice dares speak, carving poetry from pain in silver streams."

Moon's Whisper, Soul's Reply

"The moon does not demand—it invites. And the soul answers, not with noise, but with rising."

No Proof, No Pretend

"Peace isn't earned by effort or display—it waits beneath the mask you thought you had to wear."

Not the Name, Nor the Flame

"You are not the name, nor the burning of desire—you are the quiet before all longing began."

Petals of Wisdom

"A teacher does not pour knowledge—they awaken the forgotten garden already growing within us."

Phases of Becoming

"We are never broken—only in phases, like the moon, revealing more of ourselves with every turn toward light."

Reflections of the Soul

"In the mirror of each tear is the truest face we wear—unmasked, unguarded, and infinitely human."

Return to the Vastness

"To come home is not to go anywhere, but to remember—you are the vast, the still, the eternal within."

Rise from the Shadows

"In the dying whispers of the soul, hope and love weave the courage to rise and shine anew."

Rising Where Angels Tread

"Those who walk with trust ascend beyond shadows, rising to places where angels quietly tread."

Sanctuary in Stillness

"In the hush of the soul, the moonlight of truth rises—not with noise, but with knowing."

Sanctuary of Arms

"A parent's embrace is the first cathedral we enter, where love is the altar and belonging is the prayer."

Silent Pleas of the Soul

"Regrets are the shadows of dreams trapped in silence, yearning to break free and soar."

Silent Questions

"The questions you once asked now live in the air—unanswered, unforgotten, wrapped in the hush of longing."

Stillness is Wealth

"True richness is not earned, but remembered—in the silence where nothing is missing."

Strength in Frailty

"In our most fragile moments lies a hidden strength, urging us to live boldly and with heart."

Strength in Surrender

"There is courage in every tear that falls, for they rise from places words cannot reach, and hearts refuse to hide."

The Absence That Breathes

"Grief is love that has nowhere to go—so it lives on as breathless rooms, trembling walls, and a heartbeat paused in time."

The Alchemy of Tears

"What the world sees as sorrow, the soul transforms—every tear a drop of alchemy, softening scars into stories of grace."

The Applause That Empties

"When you trade truth for praise, the echoes may grow—but the voice within fades."

The Blade of Hunger

"Hunger sharpens more than appetite—it carves clarity into those brave enough to listen."

The Bridge that Shakes

"Even when the bridge beneath you shakes, trust the ground within—your soul's unwavering foundation."

The Calm Within the Storm

"Amid chaos and disguise, trust is the calm centre where the soul finds its unshakable strength."

The Child Within

"The forgotten child inside us stands strong—held by a love that knows no name or face."

The Cloak of Owed

"When we dress in what the world owes us, we forget the freedom of wearing nothing but our will."

The Compass of Quiet Light

"There is a compass in every heart, not carved in stars but shaped by quiet light—guiding us home, one breath at a time."

The Courage to Bloom Bare

"To truly bloom, one must stand unarmoured in the wind of change, trusting that the soul knows how to flower."

The Courage to Wax Again

"To rise again is not to forget the fall, but to let the fall become the soil from which you bloom."

The Dance of Discovery

"In each stranger's face, in every creature's grace, life reveals its sacred choreography."

The Dance of Shadows

"What we chase in the world are only shadows on water—vanishing the moment we reach for them."

The Death Before the Flight

"Wings are not earned in flight but in the stillness of surrender, where who we were dissolves into who we must be."

The Echo of Innocence

"A child's laughter never fades—it lives in the silence that follows, echoing through the chambers of the soul."

The Edge of Becoming

"We stand on the threshold of what was and what could be—only courage can cross the invisible bridge."

The Fragility of Love

"Love, like dew on a leaf, glistens with wonder but fades with neglect—what is not nurtured is lost to the first light."

The Garden of Illusion

"In the garden of entitlement, dreams wilt beneath the weight of imagined debts."

The Gold That Fades

"Gold without soul is glittering sorrow—a heavy crown on an empty throne."

The Grace of Letting Go

"To rise as something new, we must grieve what we once were—transformation is not a flight, but a burial followed by wings."

The Heirloom of a Mother's Touch

"A mother's kindness is not merely given—it is passed down through the pulse of stars and the silence between heartbeats."

The Hollow and the Holding

"There is a hollow only love dares to hold—a space shaped exactly like you, where we sit and remember."

The Hymn Unheard

"When the soul sings in silence, tears become its hymn—a sacred melody of all it dares to hold and heal."

The Inner Flame

"Your inner flame burns steady, a light no storm can extinguish or shadow dim."

The Inner Moon

"There is a moon within us all—its glow may be quiet, but it knows how to move oceans of emotion in silence."

The Kindness of Night

"In the stillness of night, fear softens, and the voice of love becomes a lullaby."

The Light Beneath the Silence

"When the world grows silent, the moon within speaks—guiding us gently where words cannot."

The Light That Stayed

"Though your form has gone, your light remains—guiding us like a star we cannot touch but always see."

The Longing That Remains

"She left, but the part of me that loved her never moved—it still stands, holding flowers, at a door never opened."

The Love That Waited Too Long

"I waited for the right moment, not knowing love doesn't wait for perfect timing—only honest hearts."

The Mastery Illusion

"To master life is not to control it, but to surrender with grace to its unfolding mystery."

The Mirage of Deserving

"The whisper of 'I deserve' often leads us astray—not toward truth, but toward illusion's embrace."

The Pain of Shedding

"It is not the breaking that wounds us—it's our resistance to it. For in the break lies the beauty of the bloom."

The Pain of Stagnation

"To resist change is to breathe without truly living—existence without expansion is the slowest form of sorrow."

The Past Reimagined

"The past is not a prison, but a shadow beneath love's wings—lifting us toward dawn."

The Pulse Beneath All Things

"Beyond thought and form, there is a silent rhythm—the essence that remains when all else fades."

The Risk of Silence

"Change may hurt, but silence wounds deeper—for what isn't spoken may still sink the soul."

The Sacred Fracture

"Every breaking is a doorway—each crack not a wound, but a whisper from the light urging you to grow."

The Sacred Undoing

"There is no becoming without undoing—no rising without falling into the truth beneath the form."

The Sacred Womb

"Emptiness isn't lack—it's the womb of all creation, holding the unseen like a mother holds the unborn."

The Seed's Surrender

"Only when the seed yields its shell does it become more than it ever knew—a lesson whispered in every becoming."

The Shadow of Doubt

"When doubt clouds the mind, every path seems uncertain, yet the journey begins with a single, brave step beyond fear."

The Shadow of What Could Be

"I live not in the past, but in the shadow it casts—where her smile once warmed, and my silence still echoes."

The Silence Between Us

"Some distances are measured not in miles, but in the words we never had the courage to say."

The Silence of Hesitation

"Hesitation stills the soul's dance, but within stillness lies the seed of courage waiting to bloom."

The Silent River

"Tears are not weakness—they are rivers that remember, flowing through every chapter our soul dared to feel."

The Skyward Soul

"The highest luxury is not comfort, but clarity—a soul unafraid to meet the sky with open eyes."

The Slipping Light

"Even the purest love can slip through our fingers if left untouched—its beauty demands our presence, not just our memory."

The Soul's Final Song

"As the last breath nears, the heart sings the dreams it still longs to fulfil."

The Soul's Mirror

"Sometimes, the beings we meet reflect not who we are—but who we are meant to become."

The Soul's Whisper

"There is a voice that calls beyond comfort—not to abandon you, but to reveal the vastness you forgot you held."

The Stairway of Tears

"If tears could build a bridge, we'd cross it nightly—seeking not answers, but the warmth of a familiar gaze."

The Truth We Forgot

"We left home not in distance, but in thought—and every silence since has been a call to return."

The Twilight Question

"When dusk draws near, we do not ask what we achieved—but how deeply we loved, and how gently we grew."

The Untouched Canvas

"Life's colours fade when brushstrokes are left undone; hesitation steals the masterpiece within."

The Unwritten Scripture

"Discipleship is not about following—it's about listening, within and without, until love becomes your only teacher."

The Vanishing Moment

"She left without warning, but perhaps it was I who disappeared first—into hesitation, into fear."

The Velvet Illusion

"Success may dress the body in silk, but the soul still weeps beneath the seams."

The Voice Beyond Fear

"The voice that calls from deep within is patient—waiting beyond doubt, ready to lead you home."

The Weight of Holding On

"To cling to what has passed is to anchor the soul in still waters—while the tide within longs to move."

The Weight of What If

"A million 'what ifs' haunt the silent night—echoes of courage that never found voice."

The Weightless Ache

"Tears carry the weight of love, loss, and longing—yet they fall weightless, lifting the burden the heart cannot bear alone."

The Weightless Peace

"Freedom begins where clinging ends—when we no longer ask the moment to become something else."

The Weightlessness of Acceptance

"There is a freedom in no longer resisting, a beauty in floating where life takes us—weightless, fearless, free."

The Years We Shared

"Twenty years beside her door, and I never knocked on the truth of my heart."

Trust Beyond the Noise

"True trust is quiet—not a roar, but a steady hand that lifts you through the storm's fiercest rage."

Truth in the Shimmer

"In the shimmer of sorrow lies a raw, untamed light—proof that even broken dreams still know how to shine."

Undying Flame

"Love's flame does not flicker or fade; it endures beyond pain, beyond time, beyond loss."

Unmaking to Become

"We are not sculpted into greatness—we are dissolved into it. What remains is what we were always meant to be."

Vows Beyond the Veil

"True love does not end with death—it lingers in vows whispered to the sky, kept in silence and in sorrow."

Walking Through Fire

"With trust as your guide, even the fiercest flames become a path to rise, not a place to fall."

Where Joy Doesn't Decay

"True joy isn't found in what fades—but in the space that never came, never left, and never breaks."

Where Love Meets You

"No matter where you fall, love bends to meet you—unyielding, infinite, and alive."

Whispers in Twilight

"In the quiet folds of fading light, a soul reveals its deepest truths beyond words."

Whispers of Goodbye

"The wind sighs not in anger, but in grief—carrying farewells too heavy for the heart to speak."

Whispers of Time

"Time does not flee—it lingers in the hush between heartbeats, whispering stories we still carry in our breath."

Whispers of the Loving Heart

"Love speaks softly in the silence, weaving threads of light through the darkest nights."

Womb of Wonder

"In the silent warmth of the womb, the first symphony of love is composed—wordless, eternal, divine."

Wrapped in Darkness, Born in Light

"Like the cocooned caterpillar, true growth begins where we can no longer see the way, only trust the becoming."

Yesterday's Gold

"Memories are not shadows of the past, but golden threads that bind the soul to what once bloomed in light."

Nature Symphony

Odes to the Earth

"Each leaf is a verse, each breeze a lullaby—nature does not preach, it invites. And when we listen not with ears, but with reverence, the Earth becomes scripture written in green."

- Shree Shambav

A Flame Rekindled

"In the glow of morning's grace, we find not just warmth, but the courage to burn again—with purpose, with love."

A Flight Without Destination

"Freedom isn't knowing where you're going. It's the courage to move with grace, even when the map disappears."

A Life Without Clutter

"What the bird builds with twigs, we complicate with bricks. Its lightness is not lack—but wisdom without weight."

A Rain That Remembers

"Even the softest drizzle holds the wisdom of ages—reminding us that renewal doesn't roar, it arrives quietly."

A Rain-Kissed Memory

"Grief does not pass; it becomes the air we breathe—the rain that falls when we remember, and the wind that answers when we call."

A Whisper of Hope

"In its gentle bloom, the flower carries a message: even the smallest life can change the world's mood."

Alive in the Moment

"The flower lives not in tomorrow, nor mourns the past—it opens fully only to the now."

Ashes and Seeds

"What looks like the end is often the soil from which faith is reborn."

Attachments That Undo Us

"The chains of desire bind tightly, veiling the truth—until we learn to let go, and the soul breathes freely once again."

Awakened by Light

"Oh gentle rays, you don't just rise—you awaken the forgotten corners of the soul, where hope once slept in silence."

Becoming the Bloom

"The flower does not strive to bloom; it aligns with the sun and the soil — and blooming becomes inevitable."

Becoming the Cloud

"Like a cloud, we shift, we change, we move on—never quite the same, yet always whole in the moment."

Before the Wind Blows

"Don't wait for the storm to remember what was precious—protect love while it still rests gently in your hands."

Between Light and Letting Go

"Twilight is the soft surrender of the sun—where endings do not grieve, but gently become beginnings."

Beyond Affirmation

"A thousand affirmations cannot grow a single flower in a soil of self-doubt."

Beyond the Breaking Tide

"Peace isn't found on the shore—it waits beyond the breaking tide, where surrender becomes clarity."

Beyond the Thorn

"You are not the wounds your beliefs once shaped; you are the healer who can choose to grow flowers where thorns once lived."

Bloom Where You Are

"The flower does not wait for a perfect place—it blooms where it is planted, and fills the air with meaning."

Blooming Beneath Loving Skies

"When spoken with hope, your body blooms—born of stars, cradled by loving skies."

Blueprints of the Heart

"While we search for plans and certainty, the bird trusts its beak and the wind—proof that purpose often precedes understanding."

Call My Name in Light

"To be called by the sun is not just to be seen, but to be claimed by love itself—restored, revived, and remembered."

Cloudlight & Secrets

"Even the moon hides sometimes—not in fear, but in elegance. Mystery is not absence—it's grace wearing shadow."

Dancing With the Wind

"Watch a flower in the breeze—not resisting, not clinging. It bends, it sways, it trusts the dance."

Dreams Draped in Gold

"Twilight dreams are not illusions, but truths wrapped in light—reminding us that hope often arrives in hush, not thunder."

Echoes in the Silence

"The love we offer and the love we hold return not in words, but in echoes—whispers that live beyond goodbye."

Echoes of a Flower

"A flower's voice is soft, but eternal—it whispers to the heart, 'Be gentle, but do not yield.'"

Ephemeral, Yet Eternal

"Though it fades with time, the memory of a flower lingers—proof that beauty does not need to last to be real."

Eternal Flame in the Night

"In the quiet of night, her soul speaks through wind—unseen but felt, a love that never dims."

Eternal Symphony of the Sea

"The ocean's waves, in endless ebb and flow, sing the timeless song of seasons—reminding us that change is the heartbeat of existence."

Exposed Yet Whole

"When the rain strips away our noise, it leaves behind something braver than silence: the raw honesty of peace."

Fear and Awe

Two Sides: "Fear and awe are twin flames—each illuminating the unknown, revealing battles within that teach us the true cost of attachment."

Fleeting but Eternal

"Though a flower may live but a moment, its essence lingers—beauty is not in its span, but in the way it lives fully while it can."

Flight in the Falling

"To fall is not to fail. Like the leaf, we descend not in despair but in trust—believing the sky still holds us."

From Drops to Rivers

"A mighty river begins with drops falling unseen, persistent beyond the clouds."

Golden Goodbyes

"Every ending carries its own light—fading gold against a darkening sky—reminding us that departures too can be divine."

Guided by Distant Beacons

"Stars, though light-years away, reach into our thoughts—illuminating the vastness within and beyond."

Harmony Without Pain

"Nature's unbroken rhythm carries no agony—only the gentle refrain of life unfolding in harmony, inviting us to remember our own inherent grace."

Healed by the Horizon

"The horizon does not rush us—it simply opens its arms, waiting for us to rise at our own pace."

Home in the Hush

"As the sky turns to velvet and the birds return home, I remember—peace was never far, only quiet."

Home is a Feeling

"A nest is not where life stays, but where it begins—real homes are carried within, not held in walls."

Hope in Every Drop

"The drizzle never shouts, but with each gentle fall, it writes this truth: pain passes, and morning always comes."

In the Dew We Believe

"Cherish the love that feels too delicate to last—for in its very fragility, it teaches us how deeply we can feel, and how gently we must hold."

Lessons in Letting Go

"Falling leaves don't grieve the branch—they dance with grace, teaching us how to release with beauty."

Letting Go Without Fear

"When the nest is empty, the bird does not mourn—it flies forward, for it never mistook shelter for self."

Light Beyond Darkness

"From the shadows of night emerges the dawn—a daily miracle that whispers of renewal, hope, and the relentless power of transformation."

Live Like a Flower

"Live like a flower—open to light, rooted in truth, and willing to let go, knowing even falling petals make the earth richer."

Love Without Demands

"The flower gives its fragrance freely, asks for nothing, and leaves behind joy simply by being."

Masterpiece Without Recognition

"The bird creates beauty for no gallery, no applause. In its silence, we hear the echo of sacred creation."

Moon Behind the Veil

"Veiled by clouds, the masked moon whispers secrets into the night—mystery woven into wind, dancing where silence listens."

Moonlight's Celestial Secrets

"Under the velvet sky, the universe unfolds softly—telling stories in the language of stars and shadows."

Moonlit Compass

"Let the moonlight guide your restlessness—some dreams don't shout, they shimmer quietly beneath the tides of the heart."

Mountains of Potential

"Majestic peaks stand as silent witnesses—calling us to rise, to challenge, and to unfold the infinite tapestry of our souls."

Moving with the Fog

"When nothing is clear, keep moving anyway—for even the fog bends to those who walk with faith."

Nature's Bling

"When the grass wears diamonds and petals drink the sky, we remember: beauty isn't rare—it's rainfall, received."

Nature's Perfect Rhythm

"Raindrops fall in measured grace, while the wind hums ancient hymns—nature's pulse beats steady, weaving the past into every present moment."

Nature's Silent Door

"Nature is the purest portal to peace—the moment you listen, you're already halfway home to yourself."

Nectar of Life

"In nature's purest essence, we find renewal—an elixir that awakens the deepest layers of our being."

Peace in Petals and Sky

"The earth hums a lullaby for every restless soul. In leaf, in river, in light—peace is not distant, only unnoticed."

Rain as Remembrance

"Every drop that falls is a tear unshed, a silent echo of love buried but not forgotten."

Raindrops on Skin, Peace Within

"A single drop on the face carries centuries of grace—soft enough to touch the heart, strong enough to heal it."

Realisation and Bliss

The Final Note: "After the toil and the trials, realisation dawns—the quiet bliss born from surrender, balance, and the acceptance of nature's eternal song."

Rising Again

"The fog may return, the light may fade, but so long as your heart beats forward—you will rise again."

Rooted in Letting Go

"True growth begins the moment we let go of what once held us. In surrender, we find where our roots belong."

Rootless, Yet Real

"We don't need roots to belong. Like clouds, we are free to float—and still carry the weight of meaning."

Roots Beneath the Bloom

"When watered with trust and care, fleeting love takes root—growing into something time itself cannot uproot."

Sailing Without Maps

"We are boats on a restless tide, guided not by stars but by the ache we carry and the dreams we never name."

Seeds of Thought

"Every thought you sow feeds your inner soil—choose what grows with mindful hands."

Silence Sings

"In the deepest stillness, I found not emptiness—but the soft voice of the divine, humming the song of everything I've ever loved."

Silent Grace

"A flower never speaks, yet it teaches stillness, resilience, and the soft power of being."

Silent Shapers

"In silence and softness, we carve paths no forceful roar could ever trace."

Solace in the Tree's Embrace

"Among towering sentinels, the heart finds refuge—where dreams rest easy beneath the gentle watch of ancient limbs."

Steps in the Silence

"In the quiet mist, progress is not in leaps—but in the courage to take one honest step at a time."

Strength in Fragility

"The nest, though delicate, survives the storm—not by resisting, but by bending with grace."

Strength in Stillness

"Though fragile to the eye, the flower endures storms with a quiet defiance we often forget to see."

Sunlight's Eternal Kiss

"Bathed in golden warmth, the soul ignites—a quiet blaze of bliss that fuels the spirit beyond the fleeting moment."

Symphony of the Sea

"The ocean's embrace is a healing melody—waves composing serenity that flows deep into the restless soul."

Symphony on the Rooftop

"The drizzle writes its lullaby on every roof tile—a melody of stillness, where even loneliness learns to hum."

Teaching Through Flight

"Birds raise their young not to keep them, but to release them—the truest love does not cling, it frees."

The Art of Drifting

"To drift like a cloud is not to be lost, but to trust that every wind carries a purpose unseen."

The Art of Letting Go

"When its time is done, the flower does not resist the fall—it returns to earth with the grace it once rose."

The Art of Moving On

"Where we see loss, the bird sees completion. To leave the nest is not to lose—it is to honour what it gave."

The Canvas of Becoming

"Every sunset is not just beauty—it is transformation, a moment where the sky teaches us to release with grace."

The Cycle of Life's Dance

"Our journey mirrors nature's rhythm—highs and lows intertwined, joy and sorrow flowing in the eternal dance of becoming."

The Dance of Butterflies

"Fragile wings paint stories in vibrant hues—reminding us that beauty often resides in delicate moments of flight."

The Dance of Time

"Time does not erase us; it shapes us. With every turn of the clock, a new story waits to be born from the ashes of the last."

The Depth of Stillness

"In the stillness of silent waters lies the power to move the earth itself."

The Door That Opens

"Change isn't the end—it's the space where the soul expands. Every goodbye is simply the threshold of something waiting to be loved."

The Earth's Silent Plea

"Barefoot on rugged paths, every step whispers a connection—reminding us that to walk freely is to honour the ground beneath."

The Echo of Light

"Even in the darkest hush, light waits—not in noise, but in the brave heartbeat of silent hope."

The Eternal Ripple

"Every thought, word, and action sends ripples into eternity. Live in a way that your ripples become waves of love and meaning."

The Firefly Path

"Even the smallest light can guide you home when your soul forgets the way."

The Forest of Awareness

"Awareness is a forest where each tree holds a story, each leaf whispers a truth, and every path leads to yourself."

The Fragile Warrior

"To be fragile is not weakness—it is to feel everything, to break and bloom again, with roots deeper than before."

The Garden Within

"Love is a garden that survives not on passion alone, but on the quiet tending of everyday light."

The Garden Within

"Your mind is a garden; every belief a seed. Choose wisely what you plant, for it will one day become the fragrance you offer the world."

The Garden Within

"Your thoughts are seeds, your emotions the water—tend to your inner garden and your life will bloom accordingly."

The Garden of Rebirth

"The jasmine bloomed not because the season changed, but because the boy learned to sit with his sorrow without fleeing."

The Grace of Letting Go

"As the drizzle falls, so should our fears—slowly, without struggle, surrendering to the gentle pull of grace."

The Ground Beneath

"Even when the stars are gone, the earth still holds you. Step forward—the unseen path will remember your feet."

The Lamenting Wind

"In the howl of wind and rustle of leaves, grief finds its voice—singing of love that time cannot erase."

The Language of Petals

"Each bloom is a wordless poem—tender in form, fierce in spirit, written in the ink of sunlight."

The Language of Storms

"The storms in life do not speak to your failures — they speak to your becoming."

The Last Dance of the Leaf

"Letting go is not falling—it's dancing with the wind one last time, trusting that even in descent, there is grace."

The Ocean Within

"The sea never sleeps—like the heart, it stirs beneath every silence, restless for something just out of reach."

The Poison of Pride and Jealousy

"Pride and jealousy carve paths of destruction—venoms that blind us from the delicate balance between toil and rest, suffering and bliss."

The Power of Raindrops

"We are not the roaring river, but the quiet raindrop shaping change unseen."

The Present Holds the Map

"We lose our way not in the future or the past—but in forgetting the grace of this one breath, this one moment."

The Quiet Bravery of Autumn

"The leaf does not mourn its fall; it listens to the wind, knowing that beauty exists even in surrender."

The Ripple Effect

"Your gentle ripple feeds the river that nourishes life beyond your sight."

The Rise of Petals

"Like petals kissed by the wind, we may drift—but with each fall, we find the ground that teaches us to rise again."

The River Doesn't Rush

"Like a river aligned with its source, manifestation flows when desire no longer resists purpose."

The River Within

"Change is not a storm to survive—it is a river to surrender to. Let it carry you beyond fear, into the freedom of becoming."

The River of Meaning

"Life is a river, and its purpose is not just to reach the ocean, but to nourish every field and valley along the way."

SHREE SHAMBAV

The Silent Architects

"No one taught the bird to build—yet it weaves a world with nothing but instinct and infinite trust."

The Silent Bloom

"A flower does not speak, yet it says everything—about grace, resilience, and the quiet courage to be beautiful, even when unseen."

The Silent Symphony

"When day exhales its final breath, even silence begins to sing, and the world listens in golden stillness."

The Sky Holds All Stories

"In every changing shape of the sky, there lives a forgotten story—of who we were, and who we still might become."

The Song Beneath Silence

"Close your eyes—what the world cannot say in words, the wind will sing through leaves and time."

The Soul's Cleansing

"Even the lightest rain can cleanse what storms could not—grief, anger, fear—all made gentle by a quiet fall."

The Stars Remember

"Night does not erase the day; it holds its memory in stars, reminding us that nothing truly fades."

The Storm and the Stillness

"There is a storm in every calm heart—sometimes, you don't need to fight it, only let it carry you home."

The Stream of Belief

"Each small act, like a raindrop, joins the current to carve through fear and doubt."

The Symphony of Surrender

"When you surrender to the rhythm of the universe, your life becomes music, not just movement."

The Thunder's Fierce Reminder

"Storms roar with dazzling might—a fierce yet sacred reminder that power and vulnerability coexist in the dance of life's seasons."

The Touch of Hope

"One gentle touch of light is enough to remind us—darkness was never the end, only the pause before resurrection."

The Veil of Truth

"Sometimes it is the fog, not the light, that tells us what we need to see—by hiding everything else."

The Voice in the Roots

"Out of the stillness, a song rises—from the stars, the soil, and the soul—reminding us we are never truly alone."

The Whisper of Change

"Oh, the winds are calling—not to break us, but to remind us that movement is life, and change is the soul's invitation to begin again."

The Whisper of Dawn

"Every dawn is a whisper from the universe: 'Begin again. Even broken wings can learn the sky.'"

The Whispering Universe

"The universe does not shout its secrets; it whispers them in the rustle of leaves, the dance of the wind, and the stillness of the stars."

The Wisdom in the Weave

"In each thread of straw and twig, the bird tells us: build not for forever, but for the moment that matters."

The Wisdom of Unknowing

"Not knowing is not failure—it is invitation. A foggy path asks not for clarity, but for trust."

The Wisdom of the Weightless

"It is not in holding tight, but in learning to let go, that we begin to understand the sky."

Through Fire and Rain

"In the furnace of pain and the downpour of sorrow, we are forged—not broken. We rise not despite it, but because of it."

Through the Storm

"True strength is not in resisting the storm, but in bending with the wind and still choosing to bloom."

Tides of the Soul

"Desires rise like waves—beautiful, wild, and brief—only to vanish where the horizon swallows longing."

Turning Sorrow Into Light

"When grief weighs heavy, it is the touch of golden light that teaches us how to alchemise pain into peace."

Unseen Legacy

"Not every deed demands applause—some legacies grow quietly, deep beneath the surface."

Wash the World Anew

"Let the rain fall not to flood but to rinse—our eyes, our hearts, our restless thoughts—until all feels new again."

Waves That Remember

"Love, like the sea, returns in fragments—never the same wave, yet always familiar in its ache."

When Seasons Speak

"Even as the leaves fall and time slips through our fingers, love whispers: every ending is already stitched with a new beginning."

Where Stars Drown

"Some nights, you must let the tide pull you under—only in the deep can you hear your mind truly whisper."

Where the Wind Whispers

"Sometimes the softest breeze carries the deepest call—an invitation to release, and return to something greater."

Whispers Beneath the Moon

"Beneath silver leaves and midnight wind, the trees remember stories we have forgotten how to tell."

Whispers in the Wind

"Every breeze carries the echo of dreams—soft, fleeting, yet powerful enough to shift the soul."

Whispers of the Ancient Earth

"Every breeze carries a memory, every river a secret—if you listen, nature speaks the language of eternity."

Whispers that Move Mountains

"True strength often flows not in noise, but in the whispers of steady care."

Windowpane Waltz

"Raindrops dance on glass not to be seen, but to be felt—each one a whisper reminding us how softly life speaks."

Wings of the Whispering Wind

"The wind carries more than air—it brings courage, freedom, and the gentle unburdening of fear."

Wisdom of the Storm

"Mountains whisper of patience, and storms remind us—what crashes down today will clear the skies tomorrow."

Pursuing your Dreams

Overcoming Obstacles

"The greatest obstacle is not the storm outside, but the voice within that says you cannot climb. Yet with every trembling step taken in faith, the mountain loses power, and your spirit gains its peak."

- *Shree Shambav*

Alchemy of Collapse

"Sometimes, what falls apart isn't your life—it's the illusion that was keeping your truth from emerging."

Beyond the Ledger

"Life is not a balance sheet of gains and losses — it is the grace to grow despite both."

Beyond the Roar

"When voices become a storm, don't add yours to the gale— listen to the hush that holds truth."

Breathing Space

"When the world tightens its grip, retreat into the space between your breaths."

Brushstrokes of Fate

"Each conscious choice is a brushstroke on the canvas of our becoming."

Calm Command

"True command is not in swift reaction, but in patient listening to what stillness reveals."

Clarity Before Currency

"Seek clarity, not just currency. Without clarity, even riches become cages."

Credibility Is Currency

"In a noisy world, trust is the rarest form of wealth—quiet, slow-earned, and impossible to fake."

Detachment is Dominion

"Own things fully, but let nothing own you. That is true power disguised as peace."

Earned Visibility

"Visibility without depth is noise. Depth without visibility is wisdom preparing to bloom."

Fame is Borrowed, Integrity is Owned

"Fame comes fast and leaves faster. Integrity, once earned, compounds like land."

From Seed to System

"Knowledge becomes wealth not when it is hoarded, but when it is planted, nurtured, and systemised."

From Wanting to Giving

"We heal not by grasping, but by giving — not by demanding love, but by becoming it."

Grace is a Growth Strategy

"Sometimes, the most profitable choice isn't to push harder—but to lead with grace, trust, and flow."

Inner Refuge

"In moments of hurried choice, the greatest courage is stepping back into your inner room."

Invisible Before Inevitable

"The most powerful forces in your life—compounding, trust, reputation—work in silence before they roar."

Invisible Inheritance

"Your children won't inherit your followers—they'll inherit your decisions, your values, your emotional patterns."

Invisible Wealth

"True wealth isn't what's in your vault, but what lives in your vibration, your values, and your vision."

Legacy is Planted, Not Posted

"Likes don't last, but the seeds you plant in silence will outgrow platforms and outlive popularity."

Money Is a Mirror

"How you relate to money is how you relate to your own worth. It reflects your fear, your faith, your freedom."

Platform Over Pedestal

"Your personal brand is not a pedestal—it's a platform. What you build on it will decide if it echoes or collapses."

Presence Over Performance

"The world may value your output, but your peace will depend on your presence."

Presence as Practice

"Presence is not merely being here; it is the practice of finding your centre in every passing moment."

Quiet Alignment

"True alignment is found not in motion, but in the gentle pause of awareness."

Quiet Power

"There is a power that doesn't shout. It moves quietly, earns deeply, and lasts forever. That is invisible capital."

Reclaiming the Self

"When we shed the weight of what we think we're owed, we find the wings of who we truly are."

Reputation Outlasts Revenue

"Revenue opens doors. Reputation keeps them open."

Sacred Silence

"Stillness is not emptiness, but the altar where soul and moment meet."

Scalability of Self

"Before you scale your systems, scale your self-awareness. What you build reflects who you are."

Scarcity is Inherited, Abundance is Chosen

"Scarcity is often passed down. Abundance must be reclaimed."

Surrender to Life

"Surrender is not weakness; it is the doorway through which freedom enters."

Systems Are Silent Workers

"Rest is not a pause from wealth-building. It's the proof that your systems are doing the work for you."

The Alignment Dividend

"When your work aligns with who you are, the returns aren't just financial—they're spiritual."

The Armour of Blame

"Blame may protect the ego, but it imprisons the heart."

The Cloak of Deserving

"The belief that life owes us blinds us to the truth that we owe life our becoming."

The Compass of Enough

"Without defining 'enough,' even millions will leave you feeling poor."

The Compass of Intent

"You can't reach the summit of financial freedom using someone else's map. You need your own compass: intention."

The Echo of Energy

"Money echoes the energy with which it's earned. Resentful money screams. Aligned money sings."

The Energy of Money

"Money holds no morality. It moves according to the energy, beliefs, and stories you project onto it."

The Flame Within

"You are not here to build monuments for the world to admire—you're here to tend the unseen fire that lights your own soul."

The Harvest of Invisible Work

"Invisible labour compounds like roots underground. One day, the forest appears—and they'll call you an overnight success."

The Iceberg Principle

"The value people see is just the tip. The real asset is the character, creativity, and consistency beneath the surface."

The Long Game is a Soul Game

"The long game is not just about patience—it's about purpose. If you forget why you started, time becomes weight instead of wind."

The Pause of Power

"Conquering life's currents begins when you choose stillness over impulsive flight."

The Pulse Behind the Product

"Your product may be digital, but its heartbeat must be human."

The Quiet Builder's Advantage

"While others chase attention, build your cathedral in silence. By the time they notice, it will be unshakable."

The Sacred Shift

"When you stop chasing relevance, you make space for resonance."

The Shadow Ledger

"Every financial ledger has a shadow copy: the emotional one. Heal the shadow, and the numbers follow."

The Soul of Sustainability

"What sustains you isn't scale—it's soul. Without soul, every success is a future collapse in disguise."

The Sweet Poison of Entitlement

"Entitlement whispers comfort, but binds the soul in silent sorrow."

The Time Tiller

"You're not just managing money—you're tilling time. Sow it wisely. One day, it becomes a legacy."

The Unseen Anchor

"In a world adrift, stillness becomes the unseen anchor that keeps the soul from sinking."

The Unseen Architect

"You are always building—even in silence, even in fear. The question is: Are you building with bricks of intention or impulse?"

The Unwritten Story

"The world does not owe us a story — it offers a blank page, waiting for our awakened pen."

The Wealth of Stillness

"Stillness is where your invisible capital breathes. Action builds, but stillness aligns."

Threads of Intention

"Life is not stitched by chance, but woven with threads of intention pulled through each moment."

Time as the Ultimate Investor

"Ten years of quiet mastery will outperform ten minutes of viral fame. One leaves noise. The other leaves a name."

Value Leaves a Trace

"Real value leaves fingerprints—on hearts, in systems, across decades."

Wisdom's Whisper

"Before action, let quiet rise—only then does wisdom speak without fear."

You Are the Asset

"Before you monetise your wisdom, honour it. You are the asset long before the income is."

Success and Achievements

Unleashing Your Potential

The chapters of your greatness are not written by fate, but by the ink of your effort. Turn the page. Pick up the pen. The story begins when you believe it can."

- *Shree Shambav*

Align

"When power is guided by purpose and riches are shaped by values, a life of legacy begins to unfold."

Awaken

"Real wealth is not measured in what you accumulate, but in what you awaken."

Beyond the Illusion

"Most chase riches, thinking they'll find power—only to realise the real treasure is clarity."

Bold & Transformational

"Unlearn the myths. Redefine success. Build a legacy that outlives you."

Borrowed Dreams

"Many live a life designed by expectations, not by soul. The cost is authenticity."

Build Beyond Yourself

"The powerful don't just work hard—they build systems that keep working when they rest."

Circles That Rise Together, Stay Together

"Your future is shaped by the people who speak your name when you're not in the room."

Clarity in Stillness

"In stillness, the river of life flows clearer; only then can you see the truth reflected on its surface."

Compounding the Invisible

"The most powerful things compound in silence—wisdom, trust, integrity. Invest there first."

Creators Don't Wait

"Consumers chase trends. Creators shape worlds. Your rise begins the moment you choose to create."

Direct & Inspirational

"Power. Purpose. Prosperity. Redefined from the inside out."

Earn It or Lose It

"Power imposed may win the moment, but only earned power survives the ages."

Effort Is Out, Magnetism Is In

"Real wealth doesn't chase—it calls. It's not a hunt, but a hum."

Elevated & Aspirational

"Where power meets peace, and wealth becomes wisdom."

Emotions Are the Currency

"Fear spends fast. Guilt lasts too long. Awareness creates wealth."

Failure Is a Forge

"It burns away the inessential, leaving only what's real—and unbreakable."

False Fuel

"When fear fuels ambition, success becomes exhausting instead of expansive."

False Thrones

"Power imposed without inner alignment is like a crown on a collapsing head—it dazzles, then it destroys."

Frequency is the New Currency

"You don't get what you want. You get what you are aligned with."

From Force to Flow

"Hard power may silence voices, but only soft power inspires hearts."

From Scarcity to Sovereignty

"Abundance isn't about what you own—it's about what you no longer fear."

Harmony in Action

"When your earning, saving, and spending reflect your values, the material world bows to you—not the other way around."

Holistic and Spiritual

"Rise beyond riches. Master the unseen. Live wealthy in soul and self."

Identity is the First Home

"Before you build an empire, build a self you don't want to escape from."

Illuminate

"You rise highest when your wealth echoes your why and your legacy reflects your light."

Imbalance Breeds Instability

"A man with money and no purpose is still poor. A leader with power and no peace is still lost."

In the Shadow of Gold

"Sometimes we trade everything sacred for a seat at a table that doesn't feed the soul."

Invisible Doesn't Mean Powerless

"Credibility, creativity, and consistency may not show on a balance sheet—but they write your future."

Invisible Hands

"Behind every empire stands a network—mentors, allies, and silent backers who believe before the world does."

Know What You're Building

"Rich is the sprint. Wealth is the marathon. Power is the legacy."

Learning Is Legacy

"The wealthiest minds aren't the ones that know the most—but the ones that never stop growing."

Legacy

"You don't leave a legacy by dying rich. You leave one by living richly."

Legacy Isn't Loud

"Legacy isn't what you leave behind, it's what quietly lives on in those you touched deeply."

Money Mirrors the Mind

"What you feel about money is what you attract with money."

More Than Enough

"Abundance begins the day you stop measuring your worth by what's missing."

Own Without Attachment

"Mastery begins the moment you can let go of what you own—and still take care of it."

Peace Pays Dividends

"Peace is the only investment that compounds in every area of your life."

Performing Success

"When success becomes a role you play, peace becomes a costume you forget how to wear."

Power in Stillness

"The most dangerous man is not the one who roars, but the one who has mastered the silence within."

Quiet Wealth

"Peace is wealth. Presence is luxury. Self-trust is the inheritance the world can never tax."

Release

"Every rise requires a release—of false beliefs, outdated goals, and unexamined ambitions."

Remember

"Mastery of the world means little if you are not aligned with the truth within."

Rewrite the Money Script

"You don't just earn money—you inherit beliefs about it. Heal the belief, change the outcome."

Richer Than Rich

"The richest man is not the one who has more, but the one who needs less to feel complete."

Rock Bottom Is Solid Ground

"You don't rise despite your pain—you rise because of it."

Scale the Soul

"When your knowledge becomes someone else's transformation, you've entered the realm of lasting wealth."

Social Capital Is the New Gold

"In an age of noise, trust is wealth."

Soul Debt

"Many are rich in numbers, but bankrupt in meaning—trapped in lives they bought but never chose."

Stillness Is Strategy

"Stillness is not the absence of ambition—it's the clarity that makes ambition sacred."

Stillness Is a Strategy

"Silence isn't the absence of action—it's the origin of all wise action."

Stumbles and Strength

"True living begins when we see failure not as a fall, but as the floor from which we rise."

Surrender

"Real success begins the moment your ambition bows to your calling."

Systems Are Silent Servants

"Wealth isn't just what you earn; it's what works while you rest."

The Architect Within

"Before you build anything outside, you must first redesign the blueprint inside."

The Cage Called Ambition

"When ambition is born from lack, it becomes a prison painted gold."

The Cost of the Chase

"We often trade our peace for applause, not realising silence was always the loudest success."

The Courage to Breathe Freely

"A soul unburdened by fear breathes freely; courage is not the absence of fear but the refusal to let it govern your steps."

The Creator's Mind

"Those who create from within become architects of change—while others stay renters of borrowed dreams."

The Currency of Destiny

"Consciousness, not cash, is the truest currency of the rising soul."

The Eternal Currency

"The greatest inheritance is not what you give, but what you awaken."

The Forgotten Riches

"The richest moment of your life might not be when you earn more—but when you finally feel free."

The Gift Wrapped in Ruin

"Sometimes life has to fall apart so you can rise with what truly matters."

The Hidden Empire

"Before you build the outer empire, make peace with your inner kingdom. That's where all true wealth begins."

The Illusion of Having It All

"There is no greater poverty than a full wallet and an empty soul."

The Inheritance of Scarcity

"We don't just inherit wealth or poverty—we inherit the beliefs that keep us bound to either."

The Inner Ascent

"The climb from survival to self-mastery begins the moment you stop reacting and start remembering who you are."

The Inner Economy

"You can't buy what your soul hasn't earned. True wealth is always an inside job."

The Inner Light

"The light you seek has never been outside you; it is the flicker within, waiting to blaze into a flame."

The Key to Freedom

"The weight of expectations can only shackle you if you forget that you hold the key to your own freedom."

The Mirage of More

"More isn't abundance. More can often be the hunger of what's still unloved inside you."

The Myth of the More

"More is not the answer when the ache is spiritual. No mansion fills a hollow self."

The Path of Sovereignty

"To break free from systems that control you, you must reclaim the parts of you that agreed to be owned."

The Power That Stays

"Earned power is quiet, grounded, and eternal. Imposed power needs noise to convince itself it's real."

The Power of First Light

"How you greet the morning is how you greet your life."

The Power of Positioning

"Talent gets attention. Position gets power. Learn to stand where the future is headed."

The Quiet Builders

"The ones who rise lastingly are not loud. They are anchored, clear, and move with the rhythm of their truth."

The Root Before the Rise

"You can grow fast or you can grow deep. Only one will survive the storm."

The Scarcity Cloak

"Scarcity wears ambition like armour, but fear is still what beats inside."

The Search for Peace

"You do not find peace by chasing it; you find it when you stop running from yourself."

The Shape of Freedom

"Freedom is the ability to say no, to rest without guilt, and to choose your becoming."

The Silent Currency

"Consciousness is the currency of destiny—spend it on presence, not performance."

The Silent Superpower

"Compounding doesn't shout—it builds. Slowly, silently, it makes you unstoppable."

The Soul's Balance Sheet

"Net worth means nothing if your soul's balance sheet is in deficit."

The Sovereign Mind

"Mastery is not about control over others. It's about liberation from your own chaos."

The Space Between Questions

"The most profound answers are often hidden in the spaces between our questions."

The Triangle of True Success

"Riches buy moments, wealth builds a life, and power shapes worlds."

The True Seat of Power

"The most unshakable power is the one that doesn't need to be announced—it's felt."

The Wealth Body

"The more your spirit expands, the more the world responds. Abundance is a vibration before it's a transaction."

The Wealth No One Sees

"Your calm, your clarity, and your creativity—these are fortunes far richer than gold."

The Wisdom of Silence

"Silence is not the absence of sound but the presence of wisdom; it holds the answers we cannot hear in the clamour of our thoughts."

Time Is the Truest Treasure

"Wealth is not about having more—it's about needing less and owning your time."

Truth Wears No Armour

"Authenticity doesn't need to persuade—it reveals, and that's enough."

Unshackling the Soul

"To forgive is not to forget but to unshackle your soul from the chains of yesterday."

Wealth Beyond Wallets

"Time, peace, and choice are the truest forms of wealth. Everything else is leased."

Wealth Is the Wind; Legacy Is the Seed

"Money can open doors. Character keeps them open for generations."

When Silence Leads

"In a noisy world, those who listen deeply become the most powerful voices."

When Validation Becomes Oxygen

"Chasing validation is breathing through someone else's lungs—it keeps you alive, but never whole."

Whispers of the Heart

"The heart speaks in whispers, but its truths can move mountains when we dare to listen."

You Don't Just Network—You Nurture

"The strongest connections are grown, not gathered."

Your Mind Is a Vault

"The richest person in the room is often the one who can solve a problem no one else sees."

Wisdom of Ages

Timeless Insights for Life

"Wisdom rarely shouts. It walks beside you, barefoot and calm, asking not to be followed but remembered."

- *Shree Shambav*

Anchored, Not Chained

"True power grounds you. False power grips you. One frees; the other enslaves."

Ashes Are Not the End

"The fire that consumes you is not your enemy—it is your awakening. Within every ash lies the ember of a rebirth waiting to rise."

Becoming Wealth

"You are not here to chase wealth. You are here to become it—peacefully, powerfully, and purposefully."

Beyond Fleeting Thoughts

"A passing thought cannot define you, just as a passing cloud cannot stain the sky."

Cathedral of Credibility

"No one visits the foundation of a cathedral, yet its silence holds up the beauty above. Invisible capital works the same."

Design Over Drift

"You are not a leaf on the wind—you are the architect of your becoming."

Earned Stillness

"The most successful are not the busiest, but those who have earned the right to be still and satisfied."

Echoes in the Wind

"Words left unwritten are winds that never rise—dare to speak, to write, to leave behind a storm of meaning."

Echoes of Emotion

"Regret and guilt are echoes of unspoken truths—let them fade like a fading note, not a binding chain."

Fear Is Not the Master

"Fear may knock loudly, but it has no key—it cannot enter the place where your truest self resides."

Fire Circle Wisdom

"Validation feeds your ego, but challenge feeds your evolution."

From Silence, Song

"The most profound answers do not shout—they wait for your silence to arrive before they begin to sing."

Grace in Giving

"Give with grace and trust—your quiet kindness breaks the hardest crusts of life."

Grace in Letting Go

"Letting go is not the end of a dream, but the opening of a doorway the old version of you could never walk through."

Gratitude's Whisper

"Gratitude is the soul's softest language—spoken not in grandeur, but in noticing what quietly gives us joy."

Legacy Begins Now

"Legacy is not something you leave behind. It's something you build daily—in your choices, your energy, and your truth."

Legacy is the Long Game

"When you stop building for applause and start building for time, you enter the realm of legacy."

Lessons of Light and Loss

"Life teaches with both flame and frost, asking us to feel fully—then let go gracefully."

Let the Masks Fall

"You are not your roles, your regrets, or your rehearsals—let them fall, and meet the self who watches."

Live Fully, Die Once

"Don't die before your death—let your dreams breathe, your voice echo, and your heart beat where it matters."

Not Every Fall

"You are not every stumble you've made—you are the rising, the learning, the light after the fall."

Not the Mind's Noise

"You are not the noise within your mind—you are the awareness that hears it and remains unshaken."

Pain with Purpose

"Pain, when loved and listened to, becomes the compass pointing to your highest path."

Return to the Real You

"When all else fades—fears, thoughts, labels—what remains is you: timeless, aware, and whole."

Rich, but Restless

"What's the use of riches if rest feels like a punishment and silence feels like guilt?"

Rise in Solitude

"Solitude is not absence—it is the holy ground where the next version of you prepares to rise."

Sacrifice by Default

"When you don't define richness on your own terms, you sacrifice your joy by default—for a dream that isn't yours."

Service as Legacy

"Legacy is not what you leave behind. It's what you ignite in others while you are still here."

Surrender is Strength

"True strength lies not in holding on, but in surrendering with open hands and a listening heart."

The Art in Everyone

"Everyone is an artist—not just with brush or words, but with the quiet creativity of how they love, live, and see."

The Art of Presence

"Joy isn't found in the pursuit of more—but in the reverence of what already is."

The Beginning Beneath the Pain

"Because pain is not a closing—it is a door into the deeper self, a quiet initiation into strength, truth, and rebirth."

The Breath of Wealth

"Abundance doesn't respond to desperation—it responds to presence, peace, and permission."

The Circle That Holds You

"You don't rise alone. You rise with the ones who see your light before the world does."

The Compass of Choice

"The quality of life is shaped not by circumstance, but by the precision and courage of our decisions."

The Cost of Goodness

"The horse still gets beaten, though it runs well. The tree still gets stoned, though it bears sweet fruit. Do good anyway—greatness does not shield us from trials, but gives them purpose."

The Courage to Be Enough

"Happiness isn't found in excess, but in the quiet courage to live a life of sufficiency and soul."

The Currency of Courage

"The most valuable thing you'll ever spend is your courage—invest it wisely in what sets you free."

The Discipline of Self-Trust

"When applause fades, your inner voice must rise—because the path of purpose is often walked alone."

The Enough Within You

"You are enough—not after change, not after achievement, but now, in your raw, real, unpolished presence."

The Eternity of a Moment

"Because eternity isn't measured in time—it's felt in the gravity of a single moment that changes everything."

The Exit from Survival

"You were not born to survive life—you were born to shape it with intention, meaning, and love."

The Eyes Behind Smiles

"Beware of the smile that flatters loudly; sometimes the sharpest daggers hide behind soft words."

The Foundation Beneath the Fortune

"True wealth is not built on cash, but on character. The invisible earns trust before the visible earns income."

The Freedom of Letting Go

"Freedom is found not in possession, but in surrender—in the brave stillness of having nothing left to lose."

The Gift of Letting Go

"The moment you release your ego, love flows freely from places you never expected."

The Glow Untouched

"Even when doubt wraps its fingers around your heart, your inner glow remains untouched and waiting."

The Grace of Giving and Receiving

"Do good without keeping score; receive kindness without forgetting its warmth."

The Haze of the Mind

"When the mind loses clarity, even the smallest burdens grow mountains high—yet even then, music finds its way through the fog."

The Humility That Heals

"Leave behind arrogance, and you'll find that even those who once kept their distance begin to draw near with warmth."

The Immortal Quill

"A writer dies, yet their words breathe eternally—echoing thoughts and dreams across generations long after the body rests."

The Inner Lighthouse

"Let your presence become so anchored in purpose that others find their way by your light."

The Invisible Ladder

"Some climb visible ladders—titles, trophies, trends. But the ladder that truly elevates is built within."

The Journey Inward

"Because no distance we travel matters more than the one that brings us home to who we truly are."

The Language of the Heart

"Because love speaks in pulses and silences, in presence and absence—in ways the mind cannot grasp, but the heart never forgets."

The Legacy of Living Boldly

"The greatest tragedy is not death—but a life half-lived, folded away in fear, never unwrapped by purpose."

The Light Beneath the Dark

"The darkest night cannot erase the light that lives quietly beneath—steady, waiting, eternal."

The Mirror of Praise

"Praise is a mirror—sometimes clear, sometimes distorted. Trust those who challenge you more than those who charm you."

The Mirror of Relationship

"Every relationship is a mirror—reflecting either your highest alignment or your deepest denial."

The Music of Becoming

"When you free yourself from the past, the melody of the future begins—and in that song, you find home."

The Music of Memory

"Because music holds the echoes of our past, the pulse of our present, and the longing of futures we once dreamed."

The Ocean Within

"Life will never be still like a pond. It is an ocean—learn to swim with the waves, not against them."

The Only Constant

"Cling to nothing but the music of change—for everything else drifts like smoke in wind."

The Power of Grace

"True power is not in how loudly we command, but in how gently we lead. The stronger we grow, the softer we must become."

The Power of Perspective

"Real solutions are born not from control, but from a shift in awareness—a quiet seeing beneath the surface."

The Power of Still Water

"Stillness is not the opposite of movement—it is the mother of right direction."

The Prayer of Presence

"True prayer is not in asking, but in noticing—in a soft 'thank you' whispered to every beautiful thing around you."

The Price of Pretending

"You cannot live fully when your success is a mask. Every lie you live costs a piece of your soul."

The Price of Stillness

"Still waters don't come without storms. A calm mind is built through the tempests it survives."

The Promise in Parting

"Because some goodbyes are not endings, but soul agreements to meet again—somewhere, sometime, in a softer chapter."

The Quiet Gift of Gratitude

"Happiness will never arrive for those who overlook the treasures already in their hands."

The Rise Is From Within

"No mountain, no sky, no external victory can compare to the triumph of resurrecting your own soul. The Phoenix does not chase the sun—it becomes it."

The Rise That Never Ends

"A true rise is not a peak—it is a rhythm of surrender, vision, and becoming."

The Scent of Truth

"Lies and wrongdoing may wear perfume, but truth knows—the stench of deceit can never be masked for long."

The Shapeshifting Soul

"Because the soul does not end—it simply transforms, shedding old forms to become something freer, wiser, and more whole."

The Silence Beneath the Storm

"In the chaos of thought, seek the stillness beneath—for there lies the truth untouched by turmoil."

The Silence Between Words

"Because the truest emotions don't speak—they live in the quiet between what we feel and what we dare not say."

The Silent Applause

"Consistency matters most when no one sees you. Clap for yourself when the world stays silent—be the witness to your quiet greatness."

The Soul of Joy

"Happiness lives not in grand arrivals, but in the simple presence of being surrounded by what brings you to life."

The Soul's Backward Gaze

"Because while the world rushes forward, the soul turns back—to gather what was lost, to understand what was felt, to remember what still matters."

The Spaces Where Love Lives

"Because love's deepest truths are not always spoken aloud, but breathed into the pauses, the glances, the spaces that hold us."

The Storm Beneath Stillness

"A restless mind creates chaos where none exists, but a steady soul turns turmoil into rhythm."

The Strength Within

"When the mind stands unshaken, storms become songs, and fear is woven into harmony."

The Strength in Restraint

"Power isn't proven in dominance, but in how often you choose mercy when you could have chosen might."

The Tide Called Change

"Change doesn't ask permission—it dances through all we hold dear, shaping us in its rhythm."

The Trap of Thought

"Overthinking often builds walls, not bridges. What we need isn't more noise in the mind, but clarity in the soul."

The Tree That Falls, the Seed That Rises

"Even the falling tree becomes soil for a forest not yet seen."

The True Measure of Wealth

"You don't need a million to live richly—peace, purpose, and love are more valuable than gold."

The Two Edges of Defeat

"There are only two reasons we fall—too much belief in what we are not, and too little belief in what we truly are."

The Weight of a Gentle Heart

"Strength is not in how hard you hit, but in how much you can hold without striking."

The Wick and the Flame

"What the world applauds is the flame, but it's the wick—quiet, burning within—that makes light possible."

The Wisdom of Awkwardness

"Embrace the awkward, the uncertain, the uncomfortable—it is often the birthplace of breakthroughs."

The Witness Within

"There is a watcher behind your thoughts—a calm presence that sees all and clings to none."

Trust as Currency

"In the economy of legacy, trust is the most valuable currency you'll ever hold."

Truth Over Trophies

"In a world obsessed with achievement, choosing truth is the most radical success."

Unspoken Masterpieces

"Not all masterpieces hang on walls—some live in how we forgive, how we endure, and how we love without expecting applause."

What Art Leaves Behind

"The artist may fall, but art endures—echoing through time, untouched by decay, unburied by silence."

When Enough Is Enough

"Wealth is the moment you stop asking things to make you feel whole—and you finally remember that you already are."

Where Words Fail

"In the silence where words collapse, music rises—a language carved in soul, not syllable."

Your Life, Authored

"When you stop writing from fear, your life becomes a manuscript of miracles."

Life Coach and Philanthropist

Shree Shambav is the visionary founder of the Shree Shambav Ayur Rakshita Foundation (www.shambav-ayurrakshita.org). He founded this institution with a lofty goal: to recognise human identity across gender, ethnicity, and nationality. Through this organisation, he wants to assist all communities in realising their full potential and the intrinsic beauty of life.

Shree Shambav, a Life Coach, is dedicated to supporting people on their journeys of self-discovery and empowerment. He assists people in discovering who they are, determining what inspires and drives them, and overcoming limiting ideas. His approach clarifies what one wants in life, assisting people through goal-setting and a step-by-step process for achieving them. He empowers people to make deliberate and responsible decisions, allowing them to identify their blind spots and evolve as individuals via the use of numerous strategies and tools.

The foundation's bold, uncompromising, and compassionate ventures are always aimed at initiating the "Inner Transformation" process. They focus on spiritual growth, personal growth, and self-healing while emphasising that true progress lies in "Inclusive Growth and Co-existence." This philosophy drives all their initiatives, encouraging a holistic approach to development and well-being.

Under Shree Shambav's leadership, the foundation has launched several impactful movements:

Shree Shambav Green Movement: This mission is to create a healthy, green, and clean earth through responsible water conservation and greening initiatives. The movement strives to make the world a green paradise by encouraging sustainable living and environmental responsibility.

Shree Shambav Vidya Vedhika (Vizhuthugal): This project aims to help students and children by offering training, books, stationery, and uniforms. It aims to provide the next generation with the tools and resources they need to excel both academically and personally.

Shree Shambav and his foundation exemplify the spirit of compassion, transformation, and inclusive growth via their work, which has a profound impact on individuals and communities around the world. His work exemplifies the power of acknowledging and nourishing the human spirit, creating a world in which everyone can reach their full potential and appreciate the beauty of life.

TESTIMONIALS

Journey of Soul - Karma - "We die in our twenties and are buried at eighty." Remember that nothing can stop someone who refuses to be stopped. "Most people do not fail; they simply give up." Shree Shambav deserves full credit. It allowed me to sit and consider what I might miss out on in life. The author has delved into every aspect of our daily lives. How can a seemingly insignificant change in these seemingly insignificant details bring us such joy? The Soul of Journey teaches you the "art of living" as well as the "art of dying."

Twenty + One Series - The rich cultural heritage offered a host of twenty + one short stories with incredible imagination, morals and values prevalent at a given time, influencing how people respond to a crisis or any situation. The author has recreated images with universal values and morals. The plentiful of fascinating from faraway lands would leave the modern play and story writers a cringe. The book supports trust and immeasurable values, instilling hope for the new generations.

Death - "Shree Shambav's 'Death - Light of Life and the Shadow of Death' is an extraordinary masterpiece that delves deep into the profound questions surrounding our existence and mortality. The book's opening statement, 'Nothing ever truly dies; it simply ceases to exist in one form before resuming it in another,' sets the stage for a thought-provoking exploration of death's multifaceted nature. Shambav's remarkable ability to navigate the philosophical complexities of death and our universal fear of it is both enlightening and comforting. This book is a testament to the power of understanding and acceptance."

Whispers of Eternity - "Reading 'Whispers of Eternity' by Shree Shambav was a transformative experience that left me captivated from beginning to end. Each section of this exquisite collection delves into the myriad facets of existence, offering poignant reflections on life, death, and everything in between. Shree Shambav's verses are a testament to the beauty of language and the power of expression, inviting readers to embark on a journey of self-discovery and spiritual awakening. Whether celebrating life's simple joys or grappling with the complexities of human emotion, this book is a timeless companion that speaks to the heart and soul of every reader."

Life Changing Journey Series - "Life Changing Journey Series II Inspirational Quotes" is a remarkable collection that illuminates the path to self-discovery and personal growth. With its inspiring quotes and insightful reflections, this book serves as a beacon of light in a world often shrouded in darkness. Each quote offers wisdom, guidance, and encouragement, reminding readers of their inner strength and resilience. A must-read for anyone seeking inspiration and enlightenment.

Learn To Love Yourself – "A Heartfelt Guide to Authentic Self-Love." "Learn to Love Yourself" invites readers on a transformative journey to embrace their true essence in a world often focused on external validation. Through ten insightful chapters, it gently reveals principles of genuine self-love, guiding readers to deepen their connection with themselves. Beyond surface positivity, it encourages the cultivation of resilient self-acceptance, from embracing one's unique qualities to setting empowering boundaries. With inspiring stories and practical wisdom, this book is a trusted companion on the path to inner peace, fulfilment, and joy, helping readers build lives that reflect their authentic selves.

The Power of Letting Go – This book has been a gift to my spiritual journey. Shree Shambav's insights into attachment, personal growth cycles, and forgiveness are enlightening. The concept of seven-year cycles resonated with me, helping me understand the natural phases of life. I feel more empowered to let go of what no longer serves me and step into a life of freedom and fulfilment. A truly beautiful read!

A Journey of Lasting Peace – "A Journey of Lasting Peace" feels like a trusted friend guiding you through the maze of self-discovery. The 18 transformative principles are both practical and deeply resonant, addressing everything from gratitude practices to the art of letting go. Each chapter is infused with warmth and wisdom, making it easy to apply the concepts to my life. I particularly appreciated the emphasis on physical health's connection to mental well-being; it served as a wake-up call for me to prioritise my health. This book is an invaluable resource for anyone serious about personal growth!

Astrology Unveiled Series – "Profound, Logical, and Inspiring". What stands out in Astrology Unveiled is the author's dedication to making Vedic astrology logical and approachable. Each concept flows naturally into the next, backed by examples and exercises. The insights into karma and life cycles add a philosophical depth rarely seen in astrology books. Perfect for anyone seeking spiritual growth alongside astrological knowledge!

The Entitlement Trap - "Thought-Provoking and Challenging" The book challenges readers to confront their own sense of entitlement, and that's not easy—but it's essential. The Entitlement Trap doesn't offer a one-size-fits-all approach. Instead, it's a thoughtful, layered examination of how entitlement can limit our growth. The chapter on "Defining Your Own Hill" was particularly impactful, as it pushed me to reconsider which challenges are truly worth pursuing. A thought-provoking read for those willing to do the inner work to create a life they can be proud of.

Whispers of a Dying Soul – "A Soul-Stirring Reflection on Life's Unspoken Truths" - *Whispers of a Dying Soul: Unspoken Regrets and Unlived Dreams"* is a deeply moving exploration of the unexpressed emotions and unfulfilled aspirations that shape our lives in ways we often don't realise. This book invites readers to confront the powerful, often hidden impact of regret while guiding them through a journey of introspection and healing. Each page opens a space to reflect on the choices that define us—from moments of unspoken love to neglected passions—offering a gentle reminder to live authentically and courageously.

Whispers of the Soul: A Journey Through Haiku - is a mesmerising collection that speaks directly to the heart. Each haiku is a delicate brushstroke capturing life's fleeting beauty and timeless wisdom, inviting readers into moments of deep reflection and peace. This book is a balm for the soul, guiding us to find meaning in stillness and connection in simplicity. The themes of nature, love, and mindfulness echo universal truths, resonating with quiet, powerful grace. It's a book to be savoured slowly, cherished deeply, and returned to often. Truly, it is a gift for anyone seeking calm and clarity in life's chaos.

Whispers of Silence - Unlocking Inner Power through Stillness by Shree Shambav is a rare gem that beckons readers to pause, reflect, and reconnect with their inner selves. In a world that never stops talking, this book offers a profound exploration of silence—not as a void but as a rich and transformative space.

From the first page, Shree Shambav's writing resonates deeply, blending scientific insights with spiritual wisdom in a way that feels both universal and deeply personal. The author's ability to bridge the tangible and the transcendent makes this book an invaluable guide for anyone navigating the chaos of modern life.

The Power of Words: Transforming Speech, Transforming Lives - The Power of Words is a profound and enlightening guide that has transformed the way I approach communication. Shree Shambav masterfully uncovers the hidden influence of our words on relationships, self-perception, and overall well-being. This book doesn't just teach you how to speak; it inspires mindful communication that fosters connection and trust. The insights on replacing negative patterns like gossip and judgment with kindness and authenticity are truly life-changing. The practical strategies and engaging narratives make it an invaluable resource for personal and professional growth. A must-read for anyone striving to communicate with intention, clarity, and compassion. Highly recommended!

The Art of Intentional Living: Minimalism for a Life of Purpose - "The Art of Intentional Living is a refreshing guide to finding clarity in a cluttered world. With practical wisdom and profound insights, it inspires you to simplify, prioritise, and live with purpose. A must-read for anyone seeking balance and fulfilment."

Awakening the Infinite: The Power of Consciousness in Transforming Life - "Awakening the Infinite is a transformative guide that expands the mind and nourishes the soul. With profound insights and practical wisdom, this book beautifully explores the power of consciousness, helping readers connect with their true purpose and inner potential. It is a journey of self-discovery, healing, and spiritual awakening, offering clarity and inspiration at every turn. A must-read for anyone looking to live with greater awareness, meaning, and authenticity."

Beyond the Veil: A Journey Through Life After Death:

"This book touched me in ways few others have—it's not just about death, but about life, meaning, and the vast unknown that connects them. Beyond the Veil offers a graceful blend of science and spirit, inviting us to explore the mystery with awe rather than fear. The stories, insights, and reflections linger in your heart long after the final page. A truly transformative read that brings light to the shadows of mortality. It reminded me that in embracing death, we truly learn how to live."

Bonds Beyond Blood:

"A profoundly moving story that reminds us family is not defined by blood, but by love, sacrifice, and the courage to heal. Every chapter touched my soul with its emotional truth and timeless wisdom. Through joy, grief, and redemption, this book captures the raw beauty of human connection. I saw reflections of my own family in its pages—both the pain and the hope. A powerful, unforgettable read that lingers long after the final word."

A Journey into Spiritual Maturity: 12 Golden Rules for Inner Transformation

"This book is a gentle yet powerful guide that awakened a deeper sense of purpose within me. Each golden rule felt like a mirror reflecting truths I needed to embrace. Shree Shambav's wisdom is timeless, poetic, and profoundly grounding. It's not just a read—it's a journey into the heart of who you truly are. A must-read for anyone seeking lasting peace, clarity, and inner transformation."

The Inner Battlefield: Overcoming the Enemies of the Mind and Soul:

"This book is a powerful revelation—an honest mirror to the battles we fight within. Every chapter is a step closer to clarity, peace, and emotional mastery. Shree Shambav brilliantly transforms ancient wisdom into practical guidance for modern souls. It awakened in me a new strength to face my fears and rise above inner turmoil. A must-read for anyone seeking true inner victory and lasting transformation."

The Seeker's Gold – Unlocking Life's Greatest Treasure

The Seeker's Gold is a soul-stirring masterpiece that goes far beyond the pursuit of wealth—it is a journey into the heart of what truly matters. Each chapter unfolds with poetic wisdom and emotional depth, revealing that life's real treasure is not found in riches but in the transformation of the self. As the protagonist evolves through trials, love, and profound realizations, so does the reader. This book is a mirror for every dreamer, a lantern for every seeker, and a companion for anyone walking the path of purpose. A timeless tale that stays with you long after the final page.

ACKNOWLEDGEMENTS

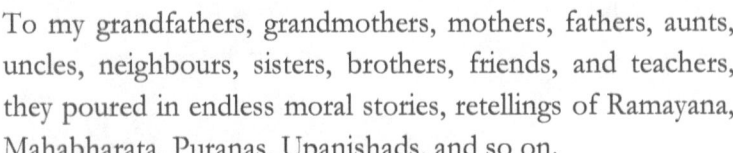

To my grandfathers, grandmothers, mothers, fathers, aunts, uncles, neighbours, sisters, brothers, friends, and teachers, they poured in endless moral stories, retellings of Ramayana, Mahabharata, Puranas, Upanishads, and so on.

My teachers, neighbours, and kindred souls. Who provided us with a stage to perform wonderful Puranic stories and were gracious enough to acknowledge our efforts.

The artists and translators of epics have served as a source of inspiration, invigorating our spirits, making these works accessible, and enabling us to grasp the profound depths and deeper dimensions they contain.

I also cherish the stimulating conversations I had with my wonderful mothers, Punitha Muniswamy and Uma Devi.

Our family's youngest member, Aadhya, who always overwhelmed me with questions, inspired this book.

I would likewise prefer to express gratitude to Mr Sivakumar, Mrs Roopa Sivakumar, Mr Akshaya Rajesh, Ms Akshatha Rajesh, Ms Apeksha Prabhu, Mr Akanksh Prabhu, Mr Nikash Sarasambi, Mrs Spoorthi Nikash for their valuable inputs.

I must thank Mr Rajesh, Mr Savan Prabhu, Mrs Revathi Rajesh, Mrs Rajani Sarasambi, and Mrs Manju Reshma, who encouraged me and often suggested writing a book. Their unwavering belief that I had something valuable to offer kept me going during my writing sessions.

Love you all,

Shree Shambav

www.shambav.org

shreeshambav@gmail.com

www.ingramcontent.com/pod-product-compliance
Lightning Source LLC
LaVergne TN
LVHW091539070526
838199LV00002B/133